The
Cave Dwellers

A PLAY IN TWO ACTS

by William Saroyan

SAMUEL FRENCH, INC.

25 WEST 45TH STREET   NEW YORK 10036
7623 SUNSET BOULEVARD HOLLYWOOD 90046
LONDON   *TORONTO*

The Cave Dwellers opened at the Bijou Theater in New York on Saturday evening, October 19, 1957. Produced by Carmen Capalbo and Stanley Chase; directed by Carmen Capalbo. It closed on Saturday, January 11, 1958, after 98 performances. The settings were designed by William Pitkin, costumes by Ruth Morley, and lighting by Lee Watson, with the following cast, in order of appearance:

THE DUKE .... *Wayne Morris*
THE GIRL .... *Susan Harrison*
THE QUEEN .... *Eugenie Leontovich*
THE KING .... *Barry Jones*
THE YOUNG OPPONENT .... *Ivan Dixon*
A WOMAN WITH A DOG .... *Vergel Cook*
A YOUNG MAN .... *John Alderman*
THE YOUNG QUEEN .... *Francine Admur*
THE FATHER .... *Gerald Hiken*
GORKY .... *Ronald Weyand*
THE MOTHER .... *Vergel Cook*
THE SILENT BOY .... *John Alderman*
THE WRECKING CREW BOSS .... *Clifton James*
JAMIE .... *Ivan Dixon*

SCENES

The play, in two acts and ten scenes, happens within the space of a few days, on the stage of an abandoned theatre on the lower East Side of New York, in the midst of a slum-clearing project.

3

INTRODUCTION

1. The Human Race

Every playwright creates a human race. The plays of Shakespeare are remembered because he created a good one; the plays of other playwrights are forgotten because they didn't.

There is no single human race for a playwright to put into his plays. He chooses any race he likes.

The truth of his race does not lie in its resemblance to the real human race. It lies in his skill as a playwright, and in his measure as a man.

Every playwright, like God, creates man in his own image. If he writes about mice, machines, angels, monsters, or men and women, they can be only in his own image.

A playwright can create his race with love, hate, humor, pity, scorn, contempt, despair, delight, regret, rejoicing, or whatever. Individual members of his human race can be embodiments of love, hate, humor, and so on, to suit the purposes of a play, but the whole play is made out of only the playwright himself. And the play is not true or false or good or bad on account of what is known and established by science through research, statistics, test, or the measurement of man—his body, his soul, his nature, his reality, and so on. It is true or false, good or bad, on account of the *art* of it.

My Heart's in the Highlands, my first play, is good or bad not because its human race is like or unlike the real human race, or any part of it. It is good or bad in its own reality, which asks for only a small area of a stage in which to suggest, or even to efface, the whole world, and fifty-five minutes of time in which to suggest, or to efface, all time.

The thing that matters is that which has been created, and that *only*. The fact that Shakespeare wrote them is not the important thing about his plays. The important thing is that they were written at all, that anybody wrote them.

In a sense, a good play is written by the human race, with one lucky or unlucky fellow doing the hard or easy work.

Bad playwriting needs the name of the playwright, if for no other reason than to let the innocent know who committed the crime.

Good playwrighting barely needs the name of the playwright—to the specialist the play itself names its playwright, to the nonspecialist his name is irrelevant.

Great playwrighting doesn't need the name of the playwright at all, since it is only another name for the human race, in any case.

The more individual the playwright the more universal the playwrighting. Nobody before or since has been anywhere near as unique, as unlike other men, as Shakespeare, and yet his plays are all men in very nearly all of the emotional, intellectual, and animal involvements and variations of human experience. Many earnest scholars believe Bacon or a Queen or a Committee wrote Shakespeare's plays. The point is irrelevant. Shakespeare equals the plays, the plays equal man, man equals the unknown and continuously to-be-revealed. The plays count and live. Shakespeare, Bacon, the Queen, and the Committee do not count. They are certainly dead.

Thus, I cannot mind that I am accused of peopling the plays I write with only myself. I wouldn't know who else to people them with. I also cannot mind that I am accused of not hating the human race. As long as I am willing to go on being a member of that race, it goes against both nature and truth for me to hate it. I cannot mind, further, that the tone of my plays is decent, as charged: that I am *with* it all, and not against it.

Without anger, annoyance, or ego; without humility, pride, or pomposity; without gladness or regret; with the impersonality in fact of one who knows he is as good as dead even while he breathes, I say that the playwrighting I have been privileged to do, have done, am doing, is not mine alone, but anybody's.

In this playwrighting there is no hysteria, not because there is none in human reality, but because there is, and because as far as I am concerned it is no longer in order. There is no emotionality, excitement, or crime; there are no heroes or villains; no right way or wrong way; no big questions, and no big answers; no shouting of protests, no cheering of righteousness.

Well, how can there be drama in such playwrighting?

By means of art, which I am not permitted to understand well enough to explain, which I am skilled enough to demonstrate in the playwrighting itself.

There is drama in my plays because they were written, because I am in them, and because I equal an order of the human race which is not unfamiliar to any other member of it.

The Cave Dwellers is only one play, but I think it will serve to demonstrate what I have been talking about.

I neither work for nor hope for the success of any of my plays. A play is already successful, in that it exists at all, and it needs no further help from me.

I am, however, interested in how a play fares, because I am interested in how anything or anybody fares. If a play fares well, I am pleased, mainly from being one who still breathes. If it fares badly, I accept that, and go about my business.

I know the greatest success can please a man only as a child is pleased; I know that the greatest success is very little, almost nothing, and nearly pitiful, were it not for health and humor; I know *all* is failure; I know the best is not much different than the worst; and I cannot mind the flourishing of the worst. The important (and wonderful) thing is that anything at all flourishes.

It is good to be a child, and to be made glad by little things, but it tends to make a fool of a man. With all my debts and taxes paid, for instance, and with money coming in all the time—from having on Broadway a little play in which nobody has any money at all—I might get confused and go out and buy myself an automobile, and a few years later wonder what I did that for. Where did I think an automobile was going to get me?

I have everything, as I always have had—wanting only the genius by which to make a little unimportant and amusing sense of the preposterous junk.

2. *The Human World*

The world itself is a cave. Here and there it is a nicely decorated cave, but the better part of it is a pitiful shambles. Man made and decorated the world, his cave, on behalf of his kids.

On behalf of the animals, on the other hand, nature made and decorated the earth, but the edges are not smooth, as they must be in the world for men, who being always so near danger and death are fussy. They want things just right. So much is wrong that they insist on having at least the details exactly right. They measure everything down to the finest point in a desperate and comic aspiration for meaning, method, and manner, whether the measuring is in architecture, dreaming, thinking, or just being.

Man is obsessed by a need or a compulsion to be picayune. He wants even God to be only his own size. He wants the universe to have limits, because his head has them. He wants time to move in a line from start to stop, because he believes he does something of the sort, starting at birth and stopping at death, neither of which he understands.

He wants the order of everything to be the order he is able to conceive.

He is unwilling even to suspect that perhaps his broadest terms are meaningless and mistaken at the outset, and that time is *not* the thing he believes it to be, a movement with light from day to night, for instance; and that space is *not* something that absolutely has got to start somewhere and stop somewhere, and so on.

Man is a limited slob, not a free one. Nature is a free slob. It isn't stingy, as man must be. It has no care for petty details. It deals in countless earths, which man hopes to count, even if the act of counting is beside the point, and only likely further to inhibit his eventual emancipation from matter, his arrival at grace.

Nature *is*—vastly, infinitely, inconceivably. But man wants to know what so much enormity means. What is it for? Vast space. Uncountable earths immeasurable distances away, existing in a silent, secret, and inconceivably simple but unknown order of action. Man also wants to know who he is. What is the earth, and what is all that crazy stuff out there in space *beyond* the earth? How long has this been going on? When and where will it stop? And so on.

Such questions are not answered in *The Cave Dwellers*. It wouldn't be a play if they were, and of course it *is* a play, and a very simple one. At the same time, however, by accident or by design—most likely by accident—a little of the *quality* of man's picayune but proud fussing comes to life in the play.

The Cave Dwellers happens on the stage of an abandoned theatre because all buildings are caves, and because the theatre is the cave at its best—the last arena in which *all is always possible*. In the caves of the government and the church, for instance, all has long since stopped being possible, in favor of a pattern of formal repetition, which some of us find only amusing and monotonous, by turns.

Two of the leading characters of the play, called the King and the Queen, are professional actors, old, unemployed, ill and comic, because apart from the truth that every man in the world is inevitably an actor of one sort or another, who else but rejected actors would find sanctuary on the stage of an abandoned theatre, with a silent and empty auditorium? Who else would return with regret and hope to a fallen empire except a King and Queen driven long ago from their own realms?

Nothing isn't allegorical, and so the play probably is, too, but you'll scarcely notice it, most likely—for which

9

let us thank a limitless God, and a universe too vast for anything to fuss over, excepting man himself, scrounging for bread and bed.

3. New York Hotels, Plays, and Playwrighting

I reached New York for the first time in August of 1928, but in those days, at the age of 20, I was not yet a hotel man. I took furnished rooms all over town from August to January, and then went back to San Francisco, still nowhere as the writer I knew I was.

I didn't return to New York until early in 1935, a few months after my first book had been published. The first hotel I stopped at was the New Yorker, but I was there only a few days, as the place was not for me. In looking for a place that was, I came at length to the Great Northern on West 57th Street, and while the rent was what I considered high, $12 a week, I took a room.

After that whenever I went to New York I stopped at the Great Northern.

In May of 1939 it was at the Great Northern that I wrote *The Time of Your Life* in six days, from Monday to Saturday.

The following year, however, I began to stop at the Hampshire House on Central Park South, both because I could afford to, and because I enjoyed the high-tone atmosphere, and the view of the Park, green or white according to the season. Over the years, now and then I stopped at a number of other hotels, too, mainly by way of finding out about them: the Plaza, the Pierre, the St. Regis, and so on.

On December 20th of 1954 when I got off a train from California and got into a taxi at Grand Central Station I asked the driver to take me to the Pierre, but on our way I told him to make it the Great Northern.

I believed I had two reasons for going back to that hotel after fifteen years: first, the rent was low; second, the offices of the City Center Theatre were across the 56th Street entrance to the hotel, and as the City Center was about to revive *The Time of Your Life*, I believed my being across the street would be convenient for me as well as for everybody else connected with the revival.

There was a third reason I wasn't aware of at the time, however. If anything, this reason was more important than the other two: I wanted to see if I might be impelled by being at the Great Northern Hotel to write a new play: and if it happened that I was so impelled, I wanted to see if I would actually write it. (Wanting to write a play and actually writing it are not the same thing.)

I *was* so impelled, and on Saturday, January 1st, 1955, I began to write the play, which for three hours was called *The End,* but after that was called *The Cave Dwellers,* as it will be forever.

As I wrote the new play, the revival cast across the street rehearsed the old one.

On Saturday, January 8th, the writing of *The Cave Dwellers* ended, but across the street the rehearsals of the old play were still in progress.

On the 19th of January, 1955, *The Time of Your Life* was performed for the first time in New York since its mid-October opening in 1939.

I considered the production a fiasco, and I still do.

All the same, the drama critics liked it, or said they liked it, and every performance was well attended.

The play grossed from twelve performances about $100,000, out of which I received travel expenses to New York, instead of 10% of the gross, or even 5%, which the City Center had been happy to pay other playwrights whose plays they had revived—a fact that came to light several months later. Too late, apparently.

Literary history, like any other kind, is supposed to repeat itself, but actually of course it never does.

The Time of Your Life was written at the Great Northern Hotel in six days, *The Cave Dwellers* in eight. There, already, is a small example of the failure of history to repeat itself. The Great Northern itself in 1939 had been at least a little less old than it had become in 1955, and so had I. Furthermore, the Tax Collector in 1939 hadn't yet decided that the reason the U. S. Government was always so sorely pressed for money was that I was spending too much for fun instead of turning it all over to him.

Still furthermore, while I was writing *The Time of Your Life* in 1939 I knew that if the producer of my first play, Harold Clurman, didn't want it (he didn't), Eddie Dowling did, sight unseen, and that it would go into immediate production; whereas, while I was writing *The Cave Dwellers* in 1955 I believed that the play would not be produced for many years.

The next time I am in New York I shall not stop at the Great Northern, not because I can afford a better hotel, but because I've been there.

But if there happens to be a playwright somewhere who is ready to write a play and is poor and hasn't yet met the Tax Collector, I can recommend that he stop at the Great Northern and write the play there.

The rent, while higher than it used to be, is still lower than the rent at other hotels. The atmosphere is decently real (that is, old but still trying to keep up appearances), the location is excellent, the Automat is just next door, Carnegie Hall is just up the street (but it isn't for visiting, it's only for walking past), the art galleries are all along 57th, Central Park is just a block and a half away. And as he does his work, the playwright can bear in mind that the writing of plays is not unprecedented in that place: the telephone operators, the desk clerks, and the bell boys will all be unobtrusive, and the engineer will be glad to fetch the playwright a worktable.

The way it goes after that is this: the typewriter is placed on the table, the playwright sits on a straight chair, and he starts to work.

If he doesn't know what to call the play, I can offer him two working titles, 1. *The Beginning,* and 2. *The End,* either of which may be changed to a more appropriate title as the play becomes written. These working titles are solely for the purpose of keeping the playwright from sitting at the desk for a week and not writing anything.

At the Great Northern Hotel the tradition is to start

writing the minute the typewriter is on the table and the playwright is on the chair. The tradition is also to write night and day, and not to take sleeping pills in order to get in a good solid six or seven hours of sleep. It is desirable for any sleeping done at that place to be light, unwilling, and only a necessary nuisance.

The eating must be of a like order—doughnuts and coffee at the Automat are lunch, beef pie and coffee are supper, and for breakfast coffee only, but as much as the playwright may wish, or have the patience to put up with, before hurrying back to work.

If work ends at three or four in the morning, a slow walk in the neighborhood is recommended, followed by a couple of shots of Irish—in 1939 it was Scotch, but times and spirits change.

It is further recommended to the playwright that he dawdle not, that it is better to write what seems to be worthless than to sit and hope (some day) to write that which will seem worthwhile.

It is also recommended that the playwright prohibit any looking forward to fame and fortune, which, if he works, will be inevitable in any case, and by that time beside the point.

It is finally recommended that before beginning to write, the playwright place paper in the typewriter.

4. *Everything and Everybody*

I have already said so many things about the theatre and plays, I don't feel like saying any more.

Instead, I will say something about everything.

There is never enough rising and spreading, seeing and knowing, in anybody, or in the whole human race, for everything ever to be *everything*. It is always only a little leap at it, and always a little pathetic. Sooner or later all such trying is seen to have been at best pompous, whether the trying has been religious, scientific, philosophical, social, aesthetic, or a little of each all at the same time.

Why this is so, anybody who wishes to do so is invited to guess.

At his best and most, man is very little. That is why the costume-formalism of diplomats at work, for instance, may so frequently seem to be suddenly theatrical, as if grave-faced kids were making up a play by means of which to feel important or to escape boredom. The impression becomes heightened when the diplomats speak, and meaning is imposed on what they say—namely, that there is no meaning in any of it.

The diplomats are playing a game.

Over the centuries has anything good come out of the diplomatic game for the human race? Or for one solitary member of it?

Possibly, but surely no better or greater good than would have been inevitable in any case, without the game.

The human race is still as fearfully sick as it was when it began, and the human race began when the animal began to ask questions, and then began to answer them. Both the questions and the answers were necessarily loaded. What he wanted, and in fact had to have, was more. He got more by asking, and still more by answering, and he grew sicker and sicker, so that now health itself is recognized as a dull form of sickness.

But what is the poor fellow to do? What can he do? What ought he to do?

There is really no answer that would not be pompous, although a smile might help a little.

I wrote *The Cave Dwellers.*

The Cave Dwellers

ACT ONE

SCENE I

The play happens on the stage of an abandoned theatre on the lower East Side of New York, in the midst of a slum-clearing project.

    There are three makeshift bunks on the stage. On one of them lies a woman called the QUEEN, *who coughs now and then in her sleep.*

    A man called the DUKE *comes in quietly, studies the face of the* QUEEN, *picks up a pile of manuscripts of old plays, dumps them in a corner, opens the top one and stands, looking at it.*

    A series of EXPLOSIONS begin, one after another, to which he half-listens.

    A GIRL *comes running down the stage alley to the stage door. She makes several unsuccessful attempts to open it, finally pushes it open, comes in, and runs to the farthest bunk, gets in, and pulls the covers over her head.*

    The DUKE *goes to the bunk in which the* GIRL *is hiding. After a moment, she puts her head out, looks around, notices the* DUKE, *looks at him out of terror-stricken eyes.*

GIRL. For the love of God, what *was* that?

DUKE. All right, now. It's only the wreckers. They're knocking down the rotten old buildings around here.

GIRL. *(Gets on her feet.)* Oh. I didn't know where to run. *(Looks around.)* Where am I?

DUKE. This is an old theatre. Here, I'll show you. This is the stage. There's the orchestra pit, out there's the auditorium, up there's the balcony. Can you see?

GIRL. Yes, now I can see all right. I've never seen a theatre from the *stage* before. It makes me feel—well, kind of proud, I guess. I don't know *why*, but it does. *(She stops suddenly and then speaks softly.)* Well, I guess I'd better go now. Thanks very much.

DUKE. That's all right.

GIRL. *(Begins to go, stops, turns.)* Of course, I'd much rather stay. Can I?

DUKE. *Here?* No, this place is for us. The Queen over there, sick. The King. He'll be back pretty soon. And me. I'm the Duke. Just names, of course. The Queen used to be on the stage. The King used to be a clown—he was in vaudeville and he did Shakespeare, too—and I used to be in the ring. We've been like a family almost a month now, and this is our home.

GIRL. Could it be my home, too?

DUKE. No, no, we've got rules and regulations. There are other places for other people.

GIRL. Where are the other places?

DUKE. All over. This is *our* place. We found it, and it's a theatre. They're going to knock it down pretty soon, but until they do we've got our— *(Softly)* rules and regulations.

GIRL. What *are* the rules and regulations?

DUKE. *People of the theatre only.* Being in the ring is being in the theatre, too, because—well, the King says so. Besides, after I lost my title, I went on tour. This isn't the first time I've been on the stage. It's just the first time that I've *lived* on one.

GIRL. Couldn't I, too?

DUKE. Are you an actress?

GIRL. Oh, no. But I *am* tired and I've got to find *some* place to stay.

DUKE. *(Looks over at the QUEEN, speaks softer.)* Well, what *have* you done?

GIRL. Well, I was at a place where they put guns together.

DUKE. What did you do there?

GIRL. I was on hammers. I never saw the *whole* gun.

DUKE. Real guns?

GIRL. I don't think so. The name of the place was U. S. Toy.

DUKE. Did the company ever put on *entertainments?*

GIRL. Not while I was there.

DUKE. At *school* did you do anything?

GIRL. *(Shakes head.)* Oh, no, I was too shy. Too shy at U. S. Toy, too.

DUKE. *Why?*

GIRL. I've *always* been shy. And afraid, too.

DUKE. Afraid of *what?*

GIRL. I don't know. Everything, I guess, and—every-*body.*

DUKE. Are you afraid of *me?*

GIRL. Well, no, but I *am* afraid I won't find a place to stay.

DUKE. Why don't you go home?

GIRL. I haven't *got* a home. *(Pause.)* Can I? Stay?

DUKE. You're young. This is no place for you.

GIRL. Please don't make me go away. I don't know why, but I don't feel so scared here. I kind of feel at home here.

DUKE. You've got to be in the theatre. The King says so, and we all agreed. He believes in the theatre. It's like a religion with him. So what am I going to tell him? Here's a scared girl? No place to go?

GIRL. Could you *teach* me to be in the theatre, maybe?

DUKE. No, that's not the same thing at all. But haven't you *ever* done anything in front of people to make them feel happy, or sad, or proud of themselves?

GIRL. I remember a sidewalk *game* that used to make *me* happy. *(Pause.)*

> One potato, two potato, three potato, four!
> Five potato, six potato, seven potato more!

DUKE. Anything else?

GIRL. *(Stands stiffly, salutes.)* I pledge allegiance to

the Flag, and to the Republic for which it stands. One nation, indivisible, with liberty and justice for all.

DUKE. *(Considers what he has heard.)* Well, you've *been* to the theatre. You've *seen* what they do. Can you do anything like *that?*

GIRL. I never went to the theatre very much—too expensive. At U. S. Toy, though, I used to *dream* a lot, and it was kind of like stuff I'd *seen* in the movies. One whole afternoon I put the hammers in upside down. Well, of course, they fired me. They almost fired another girl first, but it wasn't her. It was me.

DUKE. What were you dreaming *about?*

GIRL. Oh. *(Pause, shyly)* I don't know.

DUKE. Was it like a show on a stage?

GIRL. I don't think so, because it was only me. But I was different. I was beautiful.

DUKE. *(After thinking)* Well, I'll *tell* the King you're in the theatre. No harm in telling him, I guess.

GIRL. Will you?

DUKE. Yes. In a way you *are*. At any rate, you're *here*. And who knows? Maybe he'll believe us.

GIRL. Thank you. *(She seems anxious and afraid, as well as relieved.)*

DUKE. When I was afraid just before a fight I used to jump up and down, like this. *(He demonstrates.)* I always *wanted* to holler, too, but of course I couldn't. They'd think I was crazy. A fighter's got to be sure they don't think he's crazy. But if I'd been able to holler just before my big fight, I'd never have lost the crown. *(He looks up, whispers.)* Help me. *(He shouts.)* Help me?

    (The QUEEN *sits up, shakes her head as if to see more clearly, watches.)*

It's what I *wanted* to do. It's what I *should* have done. It's what I *never* did. What a fool I was. *(He sits down.)*

    (The GIRL *goes to him, reaches a hand out timidly, places it on his head, as a small hand on the head of a big sad dog.)*

(After a moment he looks up at her, stands.) About being in the theatre. Can you *sing*, for instance?

GIRL. *(Half sings.)* How do you do, my partner. How
do you do today?

DUKE. Not bad.

GIRL. Will you dance in a circle, if I show you the way?

QUEEN. Welcome to the theatre, Girl, whoever you are!

CURTAIN

ACT ONE

SCENE II

A little later. The GIRL *has tidied up the place. Both
unoccupied bunks are made, the tatters and rags
straightened and folded neatly. She is now sweeping
the floor. The* QUEEN *watches, sits up, rests her head
on her elbow.*

QUEEN. Well, now, where *is* the King?

DUKE. He'll be here pretty soon. Just rest now, Queen.
Sleep.

QUEEN. *More* sleep? Sleep and sleep? *(Shakes her
head.)* Remember this, Duke. And you, Girl. If I sleep
and it's time to *eat*, wake me. However deep my sleep may
be. *Lift* me *up* out of my bed if need be. Stand beside me,
one to the right and one to the left, and if I *still* sleep,
walk with me, until I am awake again. Understand?

DUKE. All right, now, don't worry. We'll wake you up.

QUEEN. You, Girl, if I sleep when it's time, you'll get
me up?

GIRL. Yes, Queen.

QUEEN. A moment ago I spoke of something. What was
it I spoke of a moment ago?

DUKE. No need to remember what you spoke of.

QUEEN. I said something. What did I say? I remembered something and then I said something. *(Sleepily)*
But now I can't remember any more. *(She falls back.)*

DUKE. *(Stands over her. Turns away, to the* GIRL.) She's asleep again.

GIRL. Shouldn't she have a doctor?

DUKE. She's old, that's all. She's been this way the whole month I've been here. And then all of a sudden she's up, and alive, and young and *beautiful*, too. There just isn't enough food that's all. She ought to have more food. *Better* food.

GIRL. I won't eat.

DUKE. You've *got* to eat.

GIRL. I'll go away, if you want me to.

DUKE. That's up to the King, now. *(The* DUKE *brings the manuscript out of his back pocket, begins to read it again.)*

(The GIRL *continues to sweep. The* KING *comes in, an old, hard, lean man with a long lined face. He is in rags, and yet he moves in a kind of human grandeur. He carries a paper sack with a round loaf of bread in it. As he moves he seems to be deep in thought. The* DUKE *and the* GIRL *wait for him to notice them, but he isn't looking.)*

KING. Enough of violence. Enough, I say. Be done with it. Have done with it.

DUKE. *(Clears his throat to attract his attention.)* King?

KING. *(Turns, almost unseeing.)* Yes? What is it?

DUKE. I looked for work all day. *Any kind.* They seem to be afraid of me, or something, that's all. I looked for money in the streets, too. I got home a little while ago to find the Queen delirious again.

KING. Enough of violence.

DUKE. What violence? Where?

KING. *In*—in—in each of us—crouched, waiting. In everything we do—and *think*, even. Enough of it. *(Softly.)* Christ, how the people hate one another to pass the beggar as if he weren't there. To be deaf to his shameful words. A small coin for a great need. *(Soberly.)* I've begged all day, begged of my inferiors.

DUKE. I hope *you've* had a little luck.

KING. This loaf of bread, old and hard, but *bread*, at any rate. *(Fishes into his pocket, comes up with a few coins, jingles them, opens his fist, looks at them.)* These few sad coins. I've begged before. Bad luck in the coins, but worse in the violence—theirs and my own. I've already called them my inferiors. Perhaps they aren't. But if they are, there's no need for *me* to say so. Enough, I'm sick of it. *(Notices the GIRL.)* Who's that standing there?

DUKE. She's in the theatre, too, like ourselves. She speaks well, and has a pleasant singing voice. *(Gestures at the beds.)* She's a helpful girl. But she's ready to go, if we don't want her.

KING. Why should the girl go? There's a whole loaf of bread. *(Goes to the GIRL.)* Welcome, Girl. And don't be afraid of me. I saw no eyes all day that were *not* afraid, and the violence of it has hurt me again, deeper than ever. In the days gone I covered this face with white grease, and red—the clown's mask. But *this* face is the mask, and the other is my true face. Welcome, and do not be afraid.

(The GIRL nods.)

(He places the coins in her hand.) Here is the whole day's gain. Buy something for the Queen. Milk, or medicine, or whatever.

GIRL. Yes, sir.

KING. *(To the DUKE.)* There were other gains. I saw a dog on a leash, held by a woman in furs. I swear that dog spoke to me with its eyes as clearly as if it had spoken with its breath and tongue and teeth and palate. *Hey, beggar! beggar! I'd give my soul to change places with you for only one turn of the world!* The woman in furs gave me nothing, not even the dirty look I've come to count on, and even to cherish a little, since I am of the theatre, and live on being seen, even if hatefully. Any kind of a look is better than none at all. The words of the eyes of the small dog were a great gain, and another was a thought that came to me soon afterwards. A bitter thought, but a true one, and so I must pass it along. When I was rich— Girl, I *have* been rich—when I wsa abroad in the world, away from the stage, and came upon a beggar—old, twisted, deformed, ugly, dirty, better than half dead— *(Stretches out his arms slowly.)* —while I was a wit in the world, a maker of wild laughter and joyous sorrow among the multitudes, did I notice the beggar? Did I *see* him, truly? Did I understand him? Did I love him? Did I give him money? *(Softly)* No, I did not. In my soul I said, *Let him be dead and out of my way. That* was a gain. *Bitter,* but a gain. Violence! My own violence, come home!

QUEEN. Oh, stop your shouting. *(She sits on the bunk, as the GIRL watches.)*

KING. Oh, you *are* awake, then?

QUEEN. Wide awake.

KING. And there's *my* bed. That makes a day. Up in the morning. Out to beg. Back in the evening. The table. The food. The company. The talk. And then to bed. *(Softly)* I love it too much.

QUEEN. Well, you're home again, at any rate, and as you see, I'm *up* again. There's one good hour in me every day, still. One good *queenly* hour. *(To the GIRL.)* I did them all, you know—Catherine, Mary, Ann, Bess, and all the others. A young girl from the most common of families, if in fact you could call it a family at all. A poor weary mother, a poor drunken father, a dirty houseful of dirty brothers and sisters. I sometimes marvel at the way I turned out.

KING. Turned out or turned in, the table's ready, if you are.

QUEEN. I have never been readier, sir.

KING. Your arm then, Woman. *(He takes her by the arm.)*

(The DUKE and the GIRL watch, and then do the same.)

CURTAIN

ACT ONE

Scene III

After supper, they are all at the table.

The King *and the* Queen *are chewing the last of the bread.*

KING. Well, that's the end of the bread.

QUEEN. *(Brightly, almost gaily)* Yes, we've eaten it all.

KING. Uptown the lights are on. The theatres are ready. The tickets are sold. The players are putting on their make-up and getting into their costumes. In a moment the curtains will go up, and one by one the plays will begin and The Great Good Friend out there— *(He gestures toward the auditorium.)* —will look and listen. And little by little something will stir in his soul and come to life—a smile, a memory, a reminder of an old forgotten truth, tender regret, kindness. In short, the secret of the theatre.

GIRL. *(Childlike)* What *is* the secret of the theatre?

QUEEN. Love, of course. Without love, pain and failure are pain and failure, nothing else. But *with* love they are beauty and meaning themselves.

GIRL. Oh.

QUEEN. *(Acts.)* Entreat me not to leave thee: for whither thou goest, I will go; and where thou lodgest, I will lodge: thy people shall be my people, and where thou diest, will I die.

KING. Bravo, you did that very well.

QUEEN. Oh, King, do a clown's bit. A *kingly* clown's bit.

KING. I belong uptown. I *still* do. I was born there, and then I was put out.

QUEEN. Are you an actor, or a sad old man like all the other sad old men? I thought it was agreed. We are of the theatre. You are to perform, not to be performed *upon*.

KING. *(Puts a crumb in his mouth.)* I'm still eating. Would you have eating a performance, too?

QUEEN. Would you have it something else? Could it possibly *be* something else? Do a bit about *eating!*

KING. We just did that bit, didn't we? *(He puts a crumb between his upper and lower teeth and crushes it with one deliberately large chomp.)*

QUEEN. This time *without* bread. For its own dear sake.

KING. I *am* challenged, Woman. You know I would kill myself for art.

QUEEN. Or *us*—from the wonder of it.

KING. *(He gets up quickly.)* The great man comes to the famous restaurant, hungry and hushed, and thoughtful, because he remembers when he was nobody and the world was still far-away. Now, he wears the unmistakable *scowl* of superiority, and so the *arrogant* headwaiter bows humbly, and conducts him quickly and silently to the best table in the place. However, before accepting the headwaiter's offer to sit— *(He indicates the drawing-out of a chair.)* —he stands a moment to notice who else has come to the holy joint, and to *be* noticed by them.

(The QUEEN *leans forward, delighted both with his work and her success in having provoked him into it.)* But who is he? *(Pause, extra clearly, now loud, now soft, inventing wildly.)* Is he perhaps the new Secretary of State, before his first flight to— *(Searches for an inept destination.) Dubrovnik?* The Spanish pianist from Palma of the Canary Islands? The man who discovered the *flaw* in the theory of cycles? He who invented the law of loss, or was it only the lollipop? Or is he perhaps the man who learned the language of the Arab tribes, brought the warring chiefs together, engineered the business of the oil? *(Slight pause.)* Let them try to guess, it's good for them. In any case, it's time to sit and eat. He eats, and eats, one rare dish after another. *(Comically astonished.)* But what's this with the crepe suzettes? A *fly,* isn't it? A *common* fly? *(He stops.)*

(The QUEEN *waits expectantly. He does not go on.)*

QUEEN. *(Softly)* Well, why do you stop?

KING. *(Earnestly)* It's part of the bit. A man stops, doesn't he? Suddenly? Unaccountably? He remembers, and he thinks, doesn't he? Is it worth it? All the *trying*, and all the eating? *(Slowly, very clearly)* Joe's dead. Mary's divorced. Johnny's boy is stealing automobiles. Pat's girl is breaking up the home of a dentist.

QUEEN. Bravo!

KING. Thank you for stopping me. I might have gone on forever, from loneliness and despair. *(Pause.)* Girl, it's your turn. Do a bit, please.

GIRL. A bit?

DUKE. *(Whispering)* The Pledge!

GIRL. *(Salutes.)* I pledge allegiance to the Flag, and to the Republic for which it stands. One nation, indivisible, with liberty and justice for all.

KING. What bit is *that*?

DUKE. The National Pledge, King!

KING. I *know* it's the National Pledge. But who the devil put it in a play?

DUKE. One of the new playwrights.

KING. Yes. They're doing that sort of thing these days, aren't they? *(Leaps to his feet, and speaks with a joyous lilt to his voice, almost singing)* Ah, Lord, what a lark it is to live! Just to live—like a mouse, even. *(He does a light skipping step and breaks into song.)*

    Jimmy Jellico, down the road,

    Come out of your house and dance with Daisy.

    Come out, my foolish, laughing, silly Jimmy.

    Your Ma is mad, your Pa is crazy,

    Come out, come out, and dance with Daisy.

DUKE. King, I didn't know you could sing, *too!*

KING. *(Softly)* Your ma is mad, your pa is crazy. *(Pause.)* And over there's the bed. I sometimes think I'm dead and have just remembered. It's most strange. And then suddenly there I am—*not* dead. And that's more strange than the other. Your turn then, Duke. A scene from a play, please.

DUKE. *(Opens the manuscript.)* The first act of a play

about some people who have come to a little hotel on a side street in a great city.

KING. Yes, yes, in search of— What *are* they in search of, Girl?

DUKE. *(Whispers, as* GIRL *turns to him for help.)* Now, just don't be *afraid*, that's all. *Tell* him.

GIRL. Well, one's looking for his father, another's looking for his mother. Another's looking for a home, another for a place to hide—

QUEEN. There *is* no hiding. None whatsoever. It can't be done.

KING. Ah, let her go on, will you? One seeks a home, another a hiding place. Go on, Girl.

GIRL. One's looking for a husband, another for a wife.

DUKE. *(Turning a page of the manuscript)* Ah, here we are. The lobby of the hotel. *(To the* GIRL.) The moment I *saw* you I was sure I knew you.

GIRL. I was sure I knew *you*, too.

KING. Is that from the play?

DUKE. Yes, King. The moment I saw you I was sure I knew you.

GIRL. I was sure I knew you, too.

QUEEN. No, no, don't go back. *Never* go back.

DUKE. But the line's repeated, Queen.

QUEEN. Ah, well, then.

DUKE. *(Acts.)* I said to myself, I know her. I've seen her before.

GIRL. I said to myself, I know him. I've seen him before.

KING. *(After a pause.)* Go on, please.

DUKE. *(Swiftly)* That's all there is. He tries to smile and be polite, and so does she, but it doesn't help, so she goes up to her room, and he goes out into the street.

KING. Another new playwright, I presume.

DUKE. Yes, sir.

KING. Very strange, I must say.

QUEEN. It's not strange at all.

KING. Nothing *happens*.

QUEEN. Nothing happens! It's the story of our lives.

KING. Yes, it is actually, isn't it? *(Pause.)* Girl?

GIRL. Yes, King.

KING. Stand before me, please.

GIRL. *(Stands there.)* Yes, King.

KING. Do not be afraid. *(Pause.)* You have a bed?

DUKE. I'd like her to have my bed.

QUEEN. *Your* bed? You'd be dead by morning without your bed.

DUKE. My clothes are warm.

QUEEN. You must be very strong and handsome inside to be able to love with so much *courtesy*.

DUKE. No, Queen. I am a slob, inside and out, and all because fifteen years ago in my last fight, I was afraid I might kill my opponent with one blow. And so, down *I* went, killed with one blow by my opponent. *(Pause.)* Whether I'm dead or alive by morning, the Girl will be safe in my bed. Courtesy, or whatever you want to call it, Queen, is like training for a big fight, anyway, except that now I can look up and holler all I like.

KING. Holler *what?*

DUKE. *(Softly but clearly)* Help me to win without killing my opponent!

CURTAIN

ACT ONE

SCENE IV

Later. STORM. WIND. The sounds of human sleeping—BREATHING, MURMURING, a HUM.

The GIRL is asleep in the DUKE'S bed. The QUEEN in her bed, and the KING in his.

The DUKE is walking up and down, to keep warm. Every now and then he shadow-boxes in silence. Stops, bundles himself in his rags, walks again. He is remembering his big fight. He walks the boundary of the fight ring, takes his corner, and waits, looking

*up now and then. The GONG is heard, but differently
—like a chime—almost an invitation to sleep. And
out of nowhere comes the charging young* OPPONENT
in trunks and boxing gloves. The DUKE *puts up his
arms and works fearfully, trying to keep away, but
suddenly the* OPPONENT *tags him. He wobbles, tries
to clinch, but is caught again, and his knees buckle.
The* OPPONENT *tags him quickly, and steps back to
watch the* DUKE *collapse. A VOICE is heard far
away whispering one, two, three, four, five six, seven,
eight . . . The* DUKE *gets to his feet, but the* OPPON-
ENT *is on him again. He tries to clinch, but fails.
Again the* OPPONENT *steps back to watch the* DUKE
collapse. The DUKE *is counted out, as he gets to one
knee. The* OPPONENT *helps him up, embraces him
quickly, pats him on the back, and goes. The* DUKE
*stands, dazed, unbelieving, and then sinks to one
knee again.*

The GIRL *sits up suddenly, notices him. Gets out
of the bunk, fully clothed. Goes to him, shyly.*

*She takes him by the arm, as if from the ring of
failure and disgrace of long ago, and helps him into
the bunk.*

The GIRL *listens to the* DUKE *as he breathes
heavily and then slowly quiets down and falls asleep.
She then wanders around in the dim light to see if
there is anything she might do, but there isn't. She
is cold, she shivers, her teeth chatter.*

*She sits on a box and begins to work in the gun
factory, doing the same thing over and over. A handsome* YOUNG MAN *comes, dancing a tango, bows to
her, they dance, and then the* YOUNG MAN *goes.*

The KING *sits up, notices the* GIRL, *gets off his
bunk, and goes to her. Takes her by the arm to his
bunk, and helps her to lie down. When she is asleep,
the* KING *begins to walk around to keep warm, too.
He then lies down and curls up like an animal, in the
hope of finding warmth, but there is no warmth in
him or in his rags or in curling up.*

A WOMAN *with a small dog on a leash appears. The* KING *gets up quickly, becomes abject, holds out his hat. The* WOMAN *stops, looks away. The dog looks up at the* KING. *The* KING'S *voice is heard whispering for the dog:* Hey, beggar! beggar! I'd give my soul to change places with you for only one turn of the world. *The* WOMAN *and the dog go.*

The QUEEN *sits up, goes to him, takes him to her bed, helps him to lie upon it, and waits until he has fallen asleep.*

The QUEEN *begins to cough, and then she sees herself as a beautiful young girl in rags, who comes and stares up at her a moment and then goes.*

The KING, *the* DUKE, *and the* GIRL *sit up at the same time, look at the* QUEEN, *and then at one another. They listen to the raging STORM. The* GIRL *goes to the* QUEEN. *The* KING *goes to the Stage Door, bolts it, places his ear to the door, and listens. The* DUKE *stands beside him.*

DUKE. We all woke up at the same time, King.

KING. Yes, I know we did.

GIRL. I dreamed a dream of love—again.

QUEEN. And I a dream of life—my own, almost gone now, swift and silent, and speechless.

KING. I saw the little dog.

DUKE. And I lost the fight. King, what's going on?

KING. We've come to a time.

DUKE. What *kind* of a time?

KING. Cold. I'm cold. (*His very voice seems frozen. He puts an arm around the* QUEEN, *another around the* GIRL.)

(*The* DUKE *does the same. They stamp their feet to keep warm, and move slowly in a small circle.*)

QUEEN. Why do you gather us into a circle?

KING. Because we can get a little warmth from one another in a circle, that's why.

QUEEN. *(Steps out of the circle, annoyed.)* No, I refuse to join that church.

KING. It's no church. It's *us*—sleepless and cold.

QUEEN. No, I refuse.

KING. We're cold, Woman, in a cold night, in a cold building, in a cold city.

QUEEN. King, you're scared. Of dying, I suppose. But for God's sake, Man, please do not let a little cold and a little fear make a fool of you. I'm cold, too, and so is she, and so is he, and for all I know this is my last night, or yours, or theirs, or anybody's, but until my mind is gone entirely, I intend to stay alive as if this were the morning of the first day, and I a young girl with the world to seek. King, I say there is no death, even though I know I shall soon be no longer among the living.

KING. What the devil are you talking about, Woman? Or have you gone mad?

GIRL. Is that from a play?

DUKE. Oh, no.

GIRL. Can I say something, then?

DUKE. Of course you can.

GIRL. Queen, it *was* warmer when you were in the circle.

QUEEN. We need a fire, then, not a philosophy. *(She coughs.)*

GIRL. You didn't cough while you were in the circle.

QUEEN. I don't want the circle to cure my cough. My cough is not an illness. It's a language I haven't learned to understand yet.

GIRL. *(To the* DUKE:) I said something. Now, you say something.

DUKE. O.K. *(To the* QUEEN:) It is better to stand together than to stand alone.

QUEEN. Duke, believe me, were you one of my own three sons, I couldn't cherish you more, but I am afraid that what you have just said can do my pride as a mother very little good.

KING. Moses Himself almost said the same thing.

QUEEN. Go ahead, then. Hang together. Circle around

like animals. Kneel and pray. Weep and moan. I'd rather freeze to death alone.

KING. Will there *never* be a woman a man can be *glad* he met?

GIRL. *(To the* DUKE, *quickly:)* I'm going to say something more. Oh, Queen, stay with us.

QUEEN. Listen, Girl. You and I invent no philosophies and no religions. We go along with the boys—until we get fed-up to here. *(She indicates her nose.)* And then we say, Boys, go on alone now, please. Kill yourselves in the name of God, or truth, or justice, or the moon, or water, or ice cream, or anything else you can think of. Kill yourselves, and then explain it to us. We'll be here waiting, and once again we'll listen to the pitiful and preposterous explanation—how you were wrong but right but wrong but right.

KING. I give up. If Christ Himself had had you around He would have sold oranges for a living.

QUEEN. I wish He *had*. Oranges are nice. I remember especially their lovely smell in the wintertime.

KING. All of the great thinkers and prophets would have forgotten their noble visions and pure dreams.

QUEEN. They *should* have. Their noble dreams and their pure visions didn't help—didn't help, Man. And *did* hinder.

KING. Hinder *what?*

QUEEN. The *real* challenge. The *only* challenge, as you know. The challenge that is in each of us. If we are nothing involved in nothing and wish to be something involved in something, let us discover how we may achieve this transformation without fear, without lies, without humiliation, without belittlement of ourselves and others, without violence. You came in from the streets not many hours ago and spoke against violence, didn't you?

KING. Oh, I am the villain of the world, and all because I am a man. Woman, I'm *cold*. I believed that with our arms about one another we might be a little warmer in our poor bodies. Now, why do you make of this simple act a crime against reason and right, thought and—theology, for instance?

GIRL. Are they acting?

DUKE. Oh, no, they're living.

QUEEN. That little circle is the mother—*and* the father —of violence.

KING. Gathering together is an act of love.

QUEEN. Not at all. It's an act of fear. Fear of others unknown to us. But who *are* they, excepting ourselves again? They aren't people from another planet. They haven't two heads to our one, four arms to our two, or another way to start and stop life. If you can't think, Man, at least try to remember. You're not cold, you're frightened. There is no danger, you're old.

KING. A whole month she lies on that bed hanging onto life by the barest thread, but tonight when I must protect my family, she becomes Joan of Arc herself, grown old.

QUEEN. Protect? There is no protection.

KING. No illness, no death, no danger, no defense, no protection. Girl, speak to your mother, please. Comfort her. She's mad, she speaks in tongues, nobody can follow her.

GIRL. It *is* cold.

QUEEN. We're agreed on that.

DUKE. We all woke up at the same time.

QUEEN. We're agreed on that, too.

GIRL. We all feel—*strange*. As if something were happening *everywhere*, not here alone.

QUEEN. The *weather* is happening everywhere.

DUKE. No, something else, Queen. I've dreamed of losing the fight before. I *lost* the fight. Why wouldn't I dream of losing it? So it can't be that. I've been in bad weather before, too, and not inside, either. Outside. So it can't be that, either. It's something else, and I'm scared to death.

GIRL. I'm not. Of anything.

DUKE. No? When you first came here you were afraid

of everything, and now you say you're not afraid of anything. How did *that* happen?

GIRL. *(Earnestly, trying to guess)* I don't know. Nothing's changed, except that I *am* here. *(Softly)* And thankful to each of you. *(To the* QUEEN:) It isn't that you're *like* my mother, as my poor mother never was, you *are* my mother. *(To the* KING:) And you my father. *(To the* DUKE:) And you—well, not my brother, and not my lover, or my husband, either, but something like *all* of them put together. *(To the* QUEEN:) He's a man. A very *kind* man. And now that I know he's scared, I love him more than ever.

DUKE. You love me?

GIRL. Yes.

DUKE. Since when?

GIRL. Since the minute I saw you, when I came out of hiding, expecting to see a whole world in ruins, and life itself breathing its last breath, and saw you instead, on this stage. Since *then*. A hundred years ago.

DUKE. *(To the* QUEEN:) Don't tell *me* something isn't happening. When I was young and strong, I was not loved. Oh, there were many, one after another, but I wasn't *loved*. I knew it, and they knew it. It was a game, nothing more, and fun while it lasted. I was false, and they were false, and there as money to spend—and pride, and power, and arrogance, and youth, and laughter. And lies to use up. I didn't care. I wore the Crown, didn't I? I'd won the title, hadn't I? *(Almost amused but also amazed.)* And then I lost the title, and they were all gone. And I was stupid. I'd *always* been stupid—just strong and swift and lucky. Don't you love me, Girl. I'm used to it.

GIRL. I love you.

DUKE. Don't pity me, either. Pity hurts worse than hatred, worse than ridicule. I'm *not* kind. When I was young and *truly* myself, and there was one like you among the others, I never so much as *saw* her. There is no kindness in me.

GIRL. *(To the* QUEEN:) I love him. *(To the* KING:) Why? Am I too good for him? Am I radiant suddenly in the middle of the night? I can't sleep. I can't rest. I can't forget. I'm cold and alone, and I don't *want* to be any more.

(Sounds of slow FOOTSTEPS, of SHUFFLING, STUM-BLING, and FALLING are heard in the alley. EVERYBODY hears the sounds, but as the sounds are faint, they do not pay very much attention to them.)

DUKE. Thank you for your love, Girl. Thank you very much, but in the morning—
    (In the alley a woman's MOAN is heard, long and drawn out.)
In the morning, Girl—
    (A man's VOICE is heard mumbling: Soon, soon now, soon.*)*
—when this strange night is over.

(There is a slow RATTLING of the bolted door, and then three KNOCKS, not very loud, and slowly. The DUKE whispers.)

DUKE. King, there's somebody out there.

(An animal MOAN is heard.)

GIRL. Who is it?
QUEEN. Open the door, King. It's somebody in need of help.
DUKE. No, let me open it. I'm scared to death, but— well, I'm the strongest here.

(He moves. The KING stops him.)

KING. How can *we* help? We have nothing here. Three beds for four people. Rags for clothes. No food. No fire. How can *we* help?
QUEEN. By not being afraid, of course.
KING. But I *am* afraid, and so are you. I don't **know**

what's out there. I'm not even sure it's human. Sometimes it sounds human, sometimes it doesn't. But even if we weren't afraid, why should *we* open the door? There's a whole world out there, full of fortunate people in their own homes, not in a hulk of a haunted theatre. Let *them* help, whoever or whatever it is. *(He listens.)* Perhaps they've gone, in any case.

(A woman's soft MOAN is heard again.)

Ah, I don't know what to make of it. Why should they come here? We're better than half-dead ourselves. How can we help? Help with *what?*

(SOUNDS.)

QUEEN. You made a human circle a moment ago. Bring *them* into that circle, as an act of love.

(SOUNDS.)

KING. I don't know who they are.

QUEEN. It doesn't matter who they are. They are in need. This is a theatre. Man, not a cave. We are people of the theatre, not animals.

(SOUNDS.)

KING. I can't argue with a woman. Let's ask one another, then, if this is what we must do. Girl, shall we open the door?

(SOUNDS.)

GIRL. Yes, King.

KING. That's *already* two against two. How about you, Duke?

DUKE. I don't know. I don't seem to be able to think any more, but if the girl *does* love me, as she says she does, and says open the door, what can I, twice her size, ten times her strength, say? I'll open the door, King.

(SOUNDS.)

KING. Well, now, it's three to one, and the last is myself, six charlatans, and half a dozen lunatics. I'll open the door.

DUKE. No, let me, King.

KING. Stand together at the edge of the stage there. It's a large theatre, and there are other places in which to hide, if need be.

(They stand together at the edge of the stage. The KING stands up straight, ready to go.)

QUEEN. King?
KING. Yes, Woman?
QUEEN. I love you, sir.
KING. You talk too much.

(The KING walks swiftly to the door, opens it, and a MAN, leaning upon it, almost falls into his arms.)

MAN. *(Whispers.)* Thank you, thank you, thank you. *(The KING supports him, helps him in. A huge black BEAR, walking upright, follows the MAN. The QUEEN, the GIRL, and the DUKE gasp. The KING turns, sees the BEAR, tries to hide behind the MAN.)* Don't be afraid of him. But for God's sake, somebody please help my wife.

(A woman's long MOAN is heard, then a CRY of a newborn baby. The MAN begins to walk toward the sound, falls upon the BEAR, who holds him up. The GIRL runs out, followed by the QUEEN.)

CURTAIN

END OF ACT ONE

ACT TWO

Scene I

Several hours later.

The BEAR *stands to one side, chained to the floor. It still moans, but softer, and sways.*
On one cot lies the MAN *asleep.*
On another lies a WOMAN, *also asleep.*
The GIRL *and the* QUEEN *are busy around the third cot, on which an infant sleeps.*
The DUKE *is gone. The* KING *is at the open Stage Door, waiting apprehensively. The* QUEEN *looks over at him now and then. The* KING *turns from the door, goes to the* BEAR, *looks at it.*

KING. *(Almost to himself:)* A moaning bear in the middle of the night? In New York City? How should I have known? Is a bear human? *(To the* BEAR:) You scared me, sir.
(The BEAR *replies with a soft moan.)*
Yes, things are much improved now. *(To the* GIRL:) And how is the child?

GIRL. Suppose we *hadn't* opened the door?

KING. God help me, I was against it. I'll never deny *that.* I thought it was—anything but a trained bear, and a human family. A trained bear has saved the life of a new man, his mother, and his father.
(The BEAR *moans.)*
You moan most fearfully, sir.
(The BEAR *moans sweetly.)*
It wasn't like that a little while ago, but then there **was** reason enough for it not to be.

37

QUEEN. You talk good sense to the bear, King. Better sense than to the rest of us.

KING. I've always loved them. I associate them with my father. You understand, Woman, I'm uneasy about how long the Duke's been gone. And I'm worried about the few coins he had with which to buy a little milk for the boy.

QUEEN. Was there enough?

KING. Enough perhaps for one bottle. A *small* bottle, most likely. I tell you, there's no money in begging any more. *(Suddenly)* What the devil's happened to him? *(He thinks a moment.)* Oh, no!

QUEEN. What are you thinking?

KING. A foul and base thought, Woman. I refuse to name it. *(Ashamed.)* Could it be—oh, no—I refuse.

QUEEN. Could it be *what?*

KING. The Duke has run off with the money?

QUEEN. Foul and base indeed. Of course not. But could he have fallen somewhere? He's not strong at all, you know. *(To the* GIRL, *who has joined them:)* A whole month, and he's had no real food—and he needs food more than we do. Could he have fallen somewhere?

GIRL. *(Wraps a shawl around her.)* I'll go look for him.

QUEEN. Well, now, let's not *all* disappear, one by one. No! He's not fallen. I'm sure of it. It was daybreak when he went out. There are few places where milk may be bought at that hour. He'll certainly be back soon, but when the milk is here, remember this—I shall be in charge. For us, *water—all* of us, including *you,* sir.

(The BEAR *nods, moans.)*

The milk's for the mother only.

KING. What about the child?

QUEEN. The mother will take care of the child, as she already has.

KING. Oh.

QUEEN. We have no bottles and no formulas, and the mother has everything.

GIRL. I have this ring. Perhaps I can sell it, and buy some—bread.

(She hands the ring to the QUEEN, *who examines it.)*

QUEEN. It's a beautiful ring, Girl.

GIRL. It *looks* real, doesn't it?

QUEEN. Terribly. And it *is*, too, but it isn't worth money. Now, there is water in the jug. We can each drink *water*, at any rate. When the mother and father are restored a little—well, who knows? Perhaps the father has money.

KING. He has a bear, no money. If he'd had money, would he have come to this door, in that storm?

QUEEN. Very well, then, a bear. Now our acting company has been enlarged by one trained bear, and—

KING. Just a minute. You're not thinking they're to stay for some time?

QUEEN. They're *here*, sir. And, as you know, they barely made it. *(Very clearly)* These people—and I include the bear—are *here*. Beyond that door, beyond this theatre, is a whole world of wealth, in which no door opened for them. Why, I don't know, and I don't care. They're here. For how long is none of my business, but while they *are* here, they *are* here, and friends, and members of the family.

(RUNNING is heard. They ALL *turn toward the door. The* DUKE, *breathless, comes in, carrying a whole wire crate containing six quart-bottles of milk. The* KING *closes the door and puts the metal bolt in place.)*

QUEEN. Bravo!

DUKE. I'm a *poor* thief!

QUEEN. Under that bed, Duke.

(The DUKE *hurries to the* MOTHER'S *bed with the crate, slides it under, and out of sight.)*

DUKE. I'll go to jail if I *must*, but they can't have back the milk. They can't have *both*.

KING. You were seen?

DUKE. I was *chased*. *(He brings out the coins.)* There were no stores open. *(He hands the money to the* KING.) A mile away, or more, I found a restaurant, but what they wanted for *one* quart was more than I had. I wanted a cup of coffee more than anything I've ever wanted in my whole life— *(He looks over at the* MOTHER, *asleep, and at the* CHILD.) —but I went out and started walking again, and there all of a sudden right in front of me was the milk wagon. *(Pause.)* The whole place is covered with snow. All of the ruins around us are covered. I mean, I cut *through* the ruins when they chased me.

KING. *Who* chased you?

DUKE. The milkman, and a boy. His son, I guess. *(Softly)* One thing I don't understand. They ran in silence. They didn't shout *stop thief!* The father was the swiftest at first, and then the son left him far behind. I'll tell you this. When I was in training for the big fight I never ran the way I did just now. I don't get it. I'll go to jail, but nobody but the mother can have that milk.

KING. You'd better have a little yourself.

DUKE. No. It's not for me. If I had stolen it for *myself*, I could never have run that well.

KING. And the boy and his father? You lost them?

DUKE. How could I lose them? We ran in snow.

KING. Hide, then. Over there.

DUKE. *Hide*, King? After I ran *that* way? No, thank you. I don't want to hide.

(FOOTSTEPS are heard, quick and light.)
Well, here he is.

(They ALL *look at one another. There is a gentle, almost polite KNOCK on the door. The* DUKE *goes to open it. The* KING *stops him.)*

KING. Wait. Wait.

DUKE. No, we waited last time. It's all right. I don't mind.

*(The DUKE opens the door, and there in the door-
way is a BOY of eighteen or nineteen, dark and grave
of face. He looks at the DUKE, recognizes him, says
nothing, and as the DUKE steps back, somewhat asking him in by that movement, the BOY comes in. He
takes his time looking around—at everybody and
everything. His eyes go back again and again to the
GIRL, but his face remains grave. Nobody says anything. The BOY passes beside each bed, looking at
each occupant, and then back at the group watching
him. He looks up to the top of the theatre, and far
out into the auditorium. He goes to the MOTHER's
bed, squats, draws out the crate, looks around at
everybody, shoves the crate back. He gets up, and
walks back to the Stage Door.)*

(Softly) I'll go with you to the police, if you like.

*(The BOY looks at him, looks at the GIRL, shakes his
head, turns and goes. EVERYBODY looks at one another.)*

Well, why didn't he speak? Why didn't he say *something?*

GIRL. He *can't* speak.

DUKE. How do you know?

GIRL. He told me so.

DUKE. How could he tell you so? He didn't say one
word.

GIRL. He told me a lot of things.

*(An EXPLOSION is heard, falling DEBRIS, and the
VOICES of the WORKERS.)*

KING. *(Straightens up, hands coins to QUEEN.)* Off to
work, then. In the snow perhaps the people will be more
generous. *(Goes to the door, stops, turns.)* I *hate* to beg.

(He goes, followed by the DUKE.)

CURTAIN

ACT TWO

Scene II

Early that afternoon. The Mother *of the infant has the child beside her in bed, the bed partly screened off. The child cries. Stops.*

Queen. Oh, what a lovely voice, what a lovely *anger* in that voice!

Mother. Oh, Mother, your love for my child makes me proud.

(The Father, *working over an open straw suitcase, brings out cymbals for the* Bear, *turns, looks, listens.)*

Father. Well, feed the boy, will you, Wife? It's a miracle the poor fellow's allive, so feed him, feed him.

Mother. *(To the* Queen:) I *love* to feed him. I never knew.

Father. So now you know.

Mother. *(To the* Girl:) Get with a man, to get your own man, like this fellow.

Queen. Soon, now, but it is still a secret.

Girl. What is?

Queen. The *Silent* Boy, of course.

Girl. No, Queen. I love the other.

Queen. The other is a boy, too, or *was,* but it is *not* him you love.

Girl. Him alone. No other.

Queen. To argue love is lovely, but the Silent Boy *is* love.

Girl. No, Queen.

Queen. Ah, then, love them both.

Girl. No, just the one, my husband.

Father. Women! It's all women here! And the secrets of them. *(To the* Bear:) All right, Gorky, to work! One, two, three—*now!*

(The Bear *strikes the cymbals together in a rhythm, as the* Father *sings:)*

Walking on my own two feet, walking, walking down the street. The street was fair, the street was sweet, walking on my own two feet. *(He stops.)* Good, Gorky. *(He gives* GORKY *a cube of sugar.)*

Now, rest a moment, while I get my coat and cap. *(He fishes into the open suitcase on the floor, brings out a coat which he puts on, and a cap, both bright and covered with buttons and bells. Another cap he puts on the* BEAR. *He goes to the women.)* Well, now, Gorky's ready again, and so am I, Wife. We'll go out and work. With luck, who knows? Perhaps a little money for a big family.

QUEEN. You've had no food. There's milk in the jug. For you and for the bear.

FATHER. After work, perhaps, if we've had luck.

(The BEAR *moans.)*

Well, perhaps a little for Gorky, then.

QUEEN. A little for yourself, too.

FATHER. I work best hungry. It's been the way of my life. *(Points.)* That child began in hunger. *She* was my bread and wine, and now she's his, too, and the both of them to me, a miracle. Great good God, I thought the door would never open. I knew you were in here, because Gorky would not leave the door. Would you, Man?

(The BEAR *moans as the* FATHER *receives a bowl of milk from the* QUEEN *and places it on the floor before* GORKY. *The* QUEEN *pours milk into another bowl, holds it out to the* MAN.)

(He shakes his head.) Ready, then, Gorky! One, two, three, now:

(The BEAR *clangs the cymbals together, as the* FATHER *and the* BEAR *walk to the far end of the stage, turn, and go straight to the Stage Door, and out.)*

Oh, I was walking down the street, walking, walking down the street. Walking on my own two feet, walking on my own two feet. The street was fair, the street was sweet, walking on my own two feet . . .

CURTAIN

ACT TWO

SCENE III

A little later. The three WOMEN, *alone. The* QUEEN *is at the table. The* GIRL *is seated on a small box beside the sleeping* MOTHER *and child, humming softly. After a moment, she sings softly in a kind of lullaby: Rock, rock, rock to sleep. A mother and a man. Rock in the dark, rock in the light. Rock in the heart the whole long night. Rock, rock, rock to sleep. A woman and a man.*

GIRL. Oh, if only I were beautiful, as she is.

QUEEN. Oh, you *will* be, don't you worry about *that*. It's the *birth* that's made her beautiful. Here. Drink this. To *his* good health. *(She thrusts bowl at the* GIRL.)

GIRL. *(Takes the bowl.) His?*

QUEEN. Yes, Girl. The silent Boy.

GIRL. How, Queen? Do I wait all my life for love, and then when it comes, do I say suddenly, Ah, no, *that* was not love, *this* is love?

QUEEN. Yes, Girl.

GIRL. No, Queen. No.

QUEEN. The Boy loves you, and you love him. He told you so better than if he had speech. And you told *him* so.

GIRL. I didn't.

QUEEN. You didn't *want* to, because you thought it was wrong. But you did. Be *glad* you did.

GIRL. How can I be glad? The Man loves me, and needs me, and only last night I *begged* him not to deny his love. How can I be glad?

QUEEN. Be glad, and never mind how.

GIRL. I'm not that kind of a woman.

QUEEN. You're the only kind. It's just that you're only beginning to learn what kind it is. To be kind to the Man is to be unkind to the Boy. Unkind to him is unkind to life, and to yourself.

GIRL. If that's true, I don't want to be kind to myself. Or to life. *(Suddenly)* I wish the Man had never stolen, and the Boy had never followed him here.

QUEEN. Why don't you thank God you love him?

GIRL. I'll never see him again, that's why. Everyone I ever loved I never saw again. And I ached and *rotted*. *(With decision.)* I love the Man. No other. I'll see *him* again.

QUEEN. You'll see the Boy again, too.

GIRL. *(Stands, looks at the* QUEEN *with terrible earnestness.)* I will, won't I?

(The QUEEN *smiles.)*

(The GIRL *seems shocked at herself.)* No, Queen. It's not true. I love only the Man, not the Boy. Let me have my poor Man, and let someone else have the fair Boy. He's not for me. He never was. Besides, my Man outran him. Oh, I was proud—until—

QUEEN. Until you saw the Boy!

GIRL. Why is that so? *How* is it so? It *is* so, but why? The way he stood there, and walked, and looked, and *understood*. Oh, thank God I'll never see *him* again. My love is too good for me. But why?

QUEEN. In the theatre, long ago, I had a part once—a girl in love as you are. And I was torn, and angry, and ashamed, and frightened, and insecure. Did I love him? Did he love me? And if I did, and if he did, would we *both* know? Or wouldn't we, and then would I lose the other, too? Or the *little* love I had for the other? Would that little be gone, too? And then nothing at all? *(Stops.)* I was very good in that part.

GIRL. And how did it turn out?

QUEEN. It was a bad play.

GIRL. Oh, no, please. How did it turn out? The Boy, of course. You loved the Boy, of course. And he loved you.

QUEEN. *(Obviously not telling the truth)* I never found out. It was the fault of the *play*. Plays are *written*. They can go *any* way.

GIRL. And which way did *that* play go?

QUEEN. The bad way. The man who wrote the play—ah, what a sad man, and yet how he could write. He came to the rehearsals, and now and then explained why this and why that, but it was all to the end that he was sad, and very troubled, and deathly sick. He drank all the time and tried to pretend he knew why the play was bad.

GIRL. Why *was* it bad?

QUEEN. He *said* it was because it was true, but that's the lie that's always told by the writers of bad plays, as if anything *weren't* true. As if one of the true may not be chosen over another. Poor man, poor lying wonderful man. He was joyous in my girl's failure. True, he said. It's true to lose, he said. He rejoiced in my wretchedness.

GIRL. Oh, no, no.

QUEEN. Oh, it was a good part, and believe me I made the most of it. I lost the Boy. I lost the Man, but the play ran and ran. Ah, you see, the playwright said, how right I was to choose the true. The people know. And all the time it wasn't so at all, it was the art of *us*, the players, that the people cherished. The play was bad, but do you know, it is still considered a *good* play? Unbelievable, and yet there it is. Why, the man who wrote it drank himself to death before the play closed. Oh, he chose the true all right. He chose hate, or hate chose him. It was his business to choose love, to write a better play, and to live to write another.

GIRL. But what happened, what happened to *you* in the play?

QUEEN. It wasn't to me, it was to *him*, the playwright. I played my part. That's my work, *our* work. We don't write them, we perform them.

GIRL. In the play what happened to you? He *said* it was true. Is the same thing going to happen to me?

QUEEN. What happened to me in the play *is* going to happen to you, too, or not, as you choose, as if *you* were writing the play, choosing from among the true, the true for you, which is the Silent Boy, who was not chosen for me by the playwright.

GIRL. How do I choose? Is it as simple as that? I love him. I'm *ashamed* that I do, but I do. So how do I choose?

What have I got to do with it? Who chose him to be the milkman's son? Who chose the Duke to go out and steal the milk? Who chose the Silent Boy to follow him here? Who chose him to come in and to look and to understand? I didn't.

QUEEN. Ah, but when he looked at you, and looked again, you, and nobody else, chose him to love you.

GIRL. And what did *he* choose?

QUEEN. And he chose to love you, as you know.

GIRL. And he went, as silently as he came, and there we are—nowhere again, nothing again.

QUEEN. He'll be back.

GIRL. Do you think so? Do you really think so? I've waited all day. Why hasn't he come back? I love him, but if he doesn't come back, *who* do I love? Do I wait, and then go looking for him?

QUEEN. He'll come looking for *you*.

GIRL. He will, won't he? That *is* the truth, isn't it? No matter what happened in the play, he will come looking for me, won't he?

QUEEN. Yes, he will. But if he doesn't—

GIRL. No, he *must*. Please don't even *think* he may not. I'm thinking *that*, and I need you to stop me.

QUEEN. Ah, well, we shall see, we shall see. *(Points.)* Rest there on the King's bed. You've had no sleep. And I shall lie here, on the lonely bed of the poor brave Duke, God help him.

CURTAIN

ACT TWO

SCENE IV

A little later. The QUEEN *is making the bed she has slept on. The* GIRL *is making the one she has slept on. The* KING *comes in. He has lost one of his shoes, and he is angry at himself.*

KING. Ah, damn me, I went out with two shoes, and I came back with one.

QUEEN. Where is the other?

KING. Just let me damn me first, please—damn me, damn me, damn me. Now what the devil am I going to do with only one shoe? How am I to get about? *(Rubbing his foot, after removing the rag of a sock.)* There ought to be a pair of shoes somewhere in this theatre. Girl, see if you can find me a pair of shoes, will you please?

GIRL. Lost your shoe? How can a man lose his shoe? His head, perhaps, his heart, his mind—how can he lose a shoe?

KING. Look for a pair of shoes, please—damn me, damn me, damn me. Where's the bear? Where's the man of the bear?

QUEEN. They're out to work. The bear crashes cymbals together, and the man sings. He wears a colored coat and cap.

KING. And the bear?

QUEEN. A colored cap.

KING. Damn me, damn me, damn me—what's the name of that bear? Don't tell me, I'll guess. Is it Lear, the great Father? Lear was once *my* name—damn me.

QUEEN. What happened to your shoe?

KING. Hatchet, rue; latchet, rue; patchet, rue; rickey —rue—wash!

QUEEN. Oh, speak, Clown!

KING. Damn me, damn me, damn me—I *am* speaking. Hatchet, latchet, patchet! Did you find me a pair of shoes, Girl?

GIRL. No, King.

KING. Damn me.

QUEEN. Will you please talk sense?

KING. The infant? The mother?

QUEEN. They're both well.

KING. The Silent Boy? Did he come back?

(The GIRL turns, and looks at the KING.)

QUEEN. No, but he will.

KING. Damn me, damn me. What name have they given the boy?

QUEEN. He's a boy, and they know it, and the boy knows it, and knows *how* a boy's a boy, and so all day he's gotten along *without* a name.

KING. Call him George. It's a nice name. Henry. That's a nice name, too. I once knew a Polish clown named Stanislaus. He never *looked* the part. Stan, that's all— Stan. Damn me, damn me, damn me. *(Suddenly)* I gambled my shoe, and lost it. Call him Frederic. There's a nice *sound* to Frederic.

QUEEN. *Gambled your shoe?*

KING. Yes, gambled my shoe, gambled my shoe. The Wreckers, knocking down the rotten old buildings, just a little off from here. I thought I'd get a coin or two, after a whole day of failure—not one coin—not one, but a small boy gave me this. I'll never see that Boy again, most likely, but one day when he's an old man, a small boy will give him something. *(He shows a yo-yo.)* The Boss of the wrecking crew out there, and ten or eleven others, white and black, at coffee time, standing around a little fire in the ruins. Call the man Patrick. It's a nice name. Ah, you all need a laugh, I said, and I need a little of that coffee, so the Boss fills a mug for me, and another worker lights me one of his own cigarettes. The snow is coming down soft, soft. I'll give you a laugh, I said. Ah, we've had our laughs all day, they said. The falling walls make us laugh. Ah, then, I said, I'll give you a tear. *(He looks over at the* MOTHER *and the sleeping infant.)* Call him Robert. It's a fine name. *You?* Give us a tear? they said. How? I'm a clown, I said. Very well, they said, give one of us a tear, just *one* of us, and *each* of us will give you a coin. But fail, Clown, and what will you give *us?* I wasn't thinking. My shoe, I said. The shoe of my right foot. Call the boy John. John's one of the nicest names of all.

QUEEN. You lost *that* bet?

KING. Ah, the world's laughing. The workers laugh. In the snow, even. I did my captured-thief bit that brought tears to the eyes of the world only a few years ago. I did the hungry man who stole the apple pie. Call the boy Richard. Ah, Richard's a fine name. He'll do well called Richard. Had I been called Richard I might have been a *chef!* I did my rejected lover bit, and all they did was laugh—but not hard enough to bring a tear to *one* eye, and every one of them has *two*. I cheated a little because I knew I was losing, and I did a little of my ridiculed-orator bit, where the man speaks most nobly and all they do is throw vegetables at him. And then a little of my bashful boy bit. Was it twenty years ago that it made everybody weep? And blow their noses? The workers only laughed. They drank coffee and smoked cigarettes and laughed. I bent down to take off my shoe, but the Boss said, Ah, keep the shoe, Clown, keep it. But I refused. I may be a shameless beggar but I am a proud clown. Damn me, damn me, damn me.

QUEEN. It was only a game. They didn't mean it.

KING. Woman, for the love of God, I *did* mean it. What the devil's happened to the world? To the workers? Not one tear in one eye. If I've lost my art, what good is my shoe?

(EXPLOSION, DEBRIS, VOICES.)

That's them. Damn me, damn me, damn me! *(Suddenly)* Ah, they even *offered* me coins, but I refused them.

QUEEN. You had no right to refuse coins.

KING. Did I have a right to fail? No, but I failed. *(He looks at his bed.)* And there's my bed.

QUEEN. Lie down, then. You've had no sleep or rest. That's why you failed.

KING. Is it, woman? Is that it?

QUEEN. Go, lie down.

KING. Oh, I long to. I *long* to, Woman. Forever, if you ask me. *(He stretches out.)* Damn me, damn me, damn me for my failure. Call the boy— Clown. *(He falls asleep.)*

CURTAIN

ACT TWO

SCENE V

An hour or two later. The KING *is still stretched out on his bed. The* BEAR *is chained to the floor. The* FATHER *is working with the* DUKE, *and the* BEAR, *in a new act. The* QUEEN *and the* GIRL *are setting the table—bread, mainly.*

FATHER. All right now, Gorky. Watch carefully. *(Puts his arms around the* DUKE.) This man is my friend. He's *your* friend. He saved our lives. Now, with the woman with a child to look after, we need this man's help. Instead of marching, music, songs and dances—*wrestling!* A man and a bear. The Duke, and you, Gorky. *(Embraces the* DUKE.) See? I embrace him—but gently, gently. Understand? He is a friend, a dear friend. We need him. In three hours of work without the woman, you and I, Gorky, earned nothing, not one coin. Oh, the weather was against us, but even in the worst weather, *with* the woman, we have always managed to earn *something. (To the* DUKE:) All right, now, don't be afraid, Duke. Gorky understands. You understand, don't you, Gorky? A friend? A very dear friend? You are to *play* at wrestling with him. You are not to wrestle in earnest. He is a man, and you are a bear, another thing.
(The BEAR *listens, turning its head this way and that, as if to get the meaning of what the* FATHER *is saying.)*
Are you ready, Duke?

(The QUEEN *and the* GIRL *stop to watch.)*

DUKE. Well, wrestling's not my line, you know. I'm ready, but I've never wrestled. A man, *or* a bear. *(Looks around.)* I wish the King were awake.
FATHER. Gorky's an intelligent man—well, I *think* of him as a man. He's stronger than ten strong men, but

he's gentle, too. A father and a brother to those he loves.

DUKE. I love Gorky, but does Gorky love me?

FATHER. Well, he's beginning to, he's *beginning* to. He senses that everybody here is a friend, but he's not sure yet. I'm teaching him now, and he learns quickly. *(Gives* GORKY *a cube of sugar. Hands one to the* DUKE.)

(The DUKE *starts to eat it.)*

No. No. Give the sugar to Gorky.

(The DUKE *steps up to* GORKY, *holds the cube of sugar out to him, but the* BEAR *doesn't take it.)*

DUKE. You see? He doesn't love me at all.

FATHER. Gorky? My boy? This is my friend. *Your* friend. Take the sugar from him.

(GORKY *is undecided.)*

Take it, Gorky.

(GORKY *does not take it.)*

DUKE. I *want* to help. We've got a child to take care of now. All day I saw all kinds of things that I wanted to *take*—for the Boy. But I lost my nerve. I took nothing.

GIRL. I'm glad. I worried that you *might* take something and that I might never see you again.

DUKE. I begged, too, but I'm a poor beggar. Prize-fighters always are. I've *got* to help, that's all. I'm not afraid of the bear. It's just that I'm not a wrestler. Couldn't we box?

FATHER. Oh, no. That is an American sport. The bear is a European. If you were to strike him one blow that hurt him a little, just a *little,* perhaps no more than an irritation, he would go mad, and he would kill. Boxing is swift and violent. He could never understand it. But wrestling is another thing. He will soon associate it with friendship and love and simple animal play. Don't be afraid.

GIRL. No, please. *I am afraid.* I love the bear, as we all

do. But the wrestling of a man and a bear—it will never seem true to the people, in any case.

(DUKE *eats the sugar cube, noisily and slowly.*)

FATHER. True or not, they love it, and it brings in money. Streets, fairs, carnivals, perhaps even the circus, at last. My problem is that I am small, no match at all for the bear, but the Duke is a big man, almost as big as a bear, and their wrestling together would make our fortune. When I wrestle, it's a joke. *(Quickly)* All right, Gorky. *(He seizes* GORKY, *tries to throw him.)*
        (The BEAR *picks him up in his arms, rocks him, kisses him, murmurs to him, puts him down gently.)*
You see? It would never do. I've tried and tried. If I were to strike him, which I have done only once, when he began to walk after a man who had kicked him, a man he would have crushed to death, Gorky *still* loved me. If I were to strike him, it wouldn't help matters any. He's never understood why I struck him, how I could do a thing like that to him—*him*—and even now, after three long years, he still broods about it. Some things he understands, and some he doesn't. He has never been able to associate that sudden violence in me with love, and yet he has gone along on faith, waiting, waiting for understanding. *(To the* DUKE:*)* If we work slowly and patiently tonight, to-morrow we will have the beginning of a great new act. We will all be working again. Now, Gorky, my father, my brother, my son, listen to me. This man is our friend. *(He embraces the* DUKE.*)*

(The KING *sits up, half-asleep, watches and listens.*)

GIRL. No. No. Something else. He is a kind man, and he will *try,* he will try *anything* that may help, but no. I'm afraid.
    DUKE. Do you love me, Girl? Is that it?
        (The QUEEN *holds out her arm toward the* GIRL, *as if to urge her to speak truthfully.)*

Because if you *do* love me, then by God the bear must love me, too.

QUEEN. Of course she loves you, Duke. We all love you. You *are* kind.

DUKE. I mean *love*, Queen. Does she love *me*, or was that last night? Another time, another story?

GIRL. I love you.

QUEEN. Wait a moment, child.

DUKE. We are all hungry and cold and lonely, but if you do not love me entirely, as foolishly as you did last night, there is no need to pretend.

GIRL. I love you.

QUEEN. Oh, wait, wait. Love speaks a strange language. Man, she *does* love you. Of course she loves you. Besides kindness, there is great handsomeness in you, which no woman could not love in men in general, and in the one man of her heart. *(She stops.)*

DUKE. Go on, Queen.

QUEEN. She is ashamed that *while* she loves you, she also loves—

GIRL. No. No.

QUEEN. —the Silent Boy. In your youth, in the days of your fame, it was so with you, too, Man. You remember. Of course you do.

DUKE. I remember, Queen. *(To the* GIRL:) Thank you for pretending, Girl, and please be glad. *Be glad.* I am your friend.

> *(The* GIRL *throws herself into his arms, sobbing. The* DUKE *smiles, as he comforts her, whispering.)*

I *am* your friend.

(The GIRL *draws away, then goes to the* QUEEN. *The* DUKE *looks around, and then goes to the* KING. *He begins to walk toward the door suddenly.)*

QUEEN. Duke?
(The DUKE *stops.)*
(She goes to him. Turns him around.) What is it, Man?

DUKE. *(As if he were saying, "I want to beg God for Grace")* I want to beg. *(He gestures.)*

QUEEN. You've had no food. Take this bread.

DUKE. Bread, Queen? *(He struggles with his emotions, looks up, speaks bitterly, powerfully.)* Give the bread to the well-fed Boy! *(Earnestly)* Oh, I'm sorry. Please forgive me. *(He hurries out.)*

FATHER. He's too old for you, Girl.

GIRL. *(Angry.)* He's *not* too old. My love is too little. No man loves as *he* loves, and yet I do *not* love him, and the Silent Boy doesn't know I'm alive. Oh, I hate love.

FATHER. Ah, you may lose them both, and find another, or two others, and lose them, too, from loving them too much or too little or something else. And still the world is there, and you're on the stage, right in the middle of everything. Love has no reason, or rightness, or way. *(He waves at his wife.)* The *Bear* loved her. I didn't, at first. The bear *hummed* when he saw her. His soul turned sweet and gentle. For me it might have been her, it might have been somebody else. The Bear decided for me, and there she is, the mother of my son, my firstborn. Of all the women in the world was *she* the only one to be the mother of my son? No, Girl. It happened. It happened, and now it's the law, and history. It's a long world, Girl. It's a big time, and love is a *word,* if you're not busy with a bear, or a boy to put on his feet.

GIRL. I want to believe in love, Queen, whether it's a word or something else.

FATHER. It's a word all right, *and* something else, too. And that's the part that's hard to follow. What else is it? *(Almost jabbering)* Well, get up, get up now, get along into another day. Love is getting along into another day, getting to work, whatever your work is. The rest of love is —who knows? What does that mean? What does it *mean?* It means I've got to teach the Bear to wrestle a big man without hurting him. And *our* big man has gone. Now, he'll come back, won't he?

QUEEN. I wonder. There were tears in the poor man's eyes.

GIRL. Tears in *his* eyes? *He* belongs here. And now he's gone, and I'm here, and I *don't* belong here. He lied for me, Queen, out of kindness and pity. What theatre have I known? One potato, two potato? Is that being in the theatre? I pledge allegiance to the Flag. Is that acting? How do you do, my partner. Is that something in an opera? I came here lost, and he found me, and helped me, and protected me. He saved my life. I've learned more since I've been here than in all the rest of the time of my life. He lied to let me stay, and I told the truth to drive him out. Queen, I'll go find him now, and just say I'm sorry for being such a truthful *dirty* liar, and then I'll go my way.

KING. *(Gets up, speaks softly.)* Well, if anyone here should be angry, it should be *me*. Angry only that we know nothing, and that we can't learn. But I am not even angry about that, Girl, and there is no need for you to be, either. This is how it is. If we were in a palace, instead of in this cave, this would be how it is. If we had everything, and *more* than everything, this would be how it is. If we loved God and God loved us, this would be how it is. And I am not angry. I cannot be angry. This is the world, this is us, this is all there is, and we do not understand.

GIRL. Then, what's it for, Father? What's it for?

KING. For *this*, *precisely* this.

GIRL. The lies, too?

KING. There are no lies. What's it *for?* It's for putting up with—with humor, if possible. Without excuses, without astonishment, without regret, without shame, without any system and order more elaborate than courtesy and love. Do not be angry at yourself for being who you are. If you *think* you are *not* truth and beauty, perhaps you are mistaken.

GIRL. Thank you, Father. I don't belong here.

KING. Nobody *belongs* here, but here we are. My father and my mother didn't *think!* No, they didn't. But even if they had, as so many have, I still wouldn't belong here, and nobody else would, either. The Bear belongs here, and all his kind. We're another creature. We know enough to know we know nothing, and it is terrible and wonderful. They know nothing but do not know that they know nothing, and it is neither terrible nor wonderful—it just is. His name is Gorky. But his mother never gave him the name. She looked at him and there he was. A bear, and not a tiger, or a rabbit, or a hawk. We think, and remember, and speak, and laugh, and sing, and dance, and *make things* of all kinds, on purpose. We do all these things because we *don't* belong here. It's not our place. It's a cave. What are we doing in a cave? We're angels. What are we doing in bodies? *(Pause.)* For some reason, we're trying our best, helplessly, to pre-tend that we *are* in them, that we *belong* in them, and that we *are* here, and that we belong here. *(He goes to the door.)* I'll go fetch my shoe, now. I failed, and I know I failed. *(He goes.)*

GIRL. I'll go now, too.

FATHER. *(Shouts.)* Ah, stay, girl! You've been a great help to my wife and son.

GIRL. He didn't come back. I thought he would. I thought he loved me.

FATHER. How do you know he doesn't?

QUEEN. He did this morning.

GIRL. This morning. How far away this morning is. And so he loved me this morning, and this is tonight, and he didn't come back. There's no reason for me to stay any longer. Goodbye.

FATHER. *(Shouts.)* Goodbye! Everybody's always saying goodbye. You've got no place to go. Before you've even left, it's already as good as another year gone by anyway, and you've come back—so stay, stay!

(There is a loud and merry KNOCK at the door. The
      QUEEN *and the* GIRL *look at one another, desperately,*
      hopefully. The FATHER *goes to the door, opens it. It*
      is the WRECKING CREW BOSS, *and a* NEGRO HELPER.*)

BOSS. *(Comes in, looks at everybody, then speaks soft-*

ly.) What's this? We knocked as a joke. People? Here? What's that over there?

FATHER. That's Gorky, my bear. And who are you, sir?

BOSS. The foreman of the wrecking crew. And the women, what are *they* doing here?

FATHER. *A moment ago* they were arguing about love. How it works and what it means. Maybe you can tell 'em. What's it mean?

BOSS. I don't know, but I know that this beautiful old building is next for the dynamite. *(He glances up, and around.)*

FATHER. The dynamite? This is a theatre, man.

BOSS. So it is, so it is, but down it comes just the same first thing tomorrow morning, along with all the other buildings in this area. Rooming houses, offices, stores, churches—all old, all rotted, all finished—to make way for the new. But I've loved every poor old wreck of a place that my men and I have brought down. Look up there, Jamie—it's a *high* and handsome place, now, isn't it?

FATHER. Yes, while you're at it, Jamie, look over there. That's my wife. She became a mother early this morning. Beside her is my son. They can't be moved now. They need time.

BOSS. *(Near a box.)* May I sit down? I have a longing to sit down in here.

QUEEN. Welcome, sir.

BOSS. *(Looking at her strangely)* Thank you. *(Looks at the GIRL, as he sits.)* And the girl there? She's your daughter?

QUEEN. In a manner of speaking.

BOSS. What manner is that?

QUEEN. For three months short of a year an old man of the theatre and I have lived here. He found this theatre in the morning, and I found it in the afternoon. He called me the Queen, and I called him the King. Then, a month ago, an old prize-fighter found this place, and yesterday this girl found it. All in all, a family—a great Clown begging as a free man in the human streets rather than leave the theatre, and me and the prizefighter, and this Girl, who *is* my daughter.

Boss. A great *Clown? (Looks at* Jamie.) How many shoes does he wear?

Queen. Two when he has two, but now he has one.

Boss. We know the man. This afternoon he made us roar with laughter. Madam, what is your problem?

Queen. *Mine,* sir? I have no problem.

Boss. The problem of your family, then?

Queen. Love, of course. Survival, and love. And what is *your* problem, sir?

Boss. How best, swiftest, most safely, and least expensively to bring this—mansion—down into ruins, and then to clear away the debris.

Queen. Simple.

Boss. *(Holding a crust of bread)* May I?

Queen. Please, sir. And something to drink?

Boss. No, thanks, just this bread. I am confused, and my teeth need something to work upon. I'm poor at words, and at *thinking,* too, if you ask me. *(He chews.)* Jamie, boy?

Jamie. Yes, sir?

Boss. What can we do, Jamie?

Jamie. I could go find the Old Man and give him back his shoe. I've kept it in a safe place, but he could never find it. I just thought it ought to be kept in a safe place.

Boss. The mother and the child can't be moved, Jamie.

Jamie. No, sir, they can't.

Boss. Tomorrow's Friday, and the day after is Saturday, and then Sunday. *(He thinks a moment, and then speaks suddenly.)* Jamie, tell my boys, tell my crew, tell them all at once and one by one, do you hear, Jamie?

Jamie. Yes, sir.

Boss. All at once and one by one, Boys, he says we're all to be sick tomorrow, and the day after. Use the name you have for me among you; I don't mind— I've only pretended to mind. Tell them the Madman says we're all to be sick tomorrow, and the day after. That's all. Just sick. Every one of us. At home. In bed. Coughing, and

sweating. I want to study this problem *carefully*. It may
take me a little time.

JAMIE. Yes, sir.

Boss. And Jamie?

JAMIE. Yes, sir.

Boss. *(Brings money from his pocket.)* Find the Great
Man, and give him back his shoe, and then step into that
little store we all go to at lunchtime. Buy us—well, you
know, Jamie, the things we like—but a lot of it. I'm very
hungry.

JAMIE. Yes, sir. Everybody sick until Monday morning.

Boss. Jamie?

JAMIE. Yes, sir.

Boss. If anybody asks why— *(He waits a long time,
shakes his head quickly.)* There is no why.

JAMIE. Yes, sir.

(JAMIE *turns and goes quickly, as the* Boss *keeps chewing
bread.)*

QUEEN. *I'd* like to ask why.

Boss. *(Looking around from one to the other)* The
truth?

QUEEN. If you know the truth, sir.

Boss. I know, Queen. The King came by as we stopped
for coffee and cigarettes this afternoon. He said he would
make us laugh—for a coin. And my men said, Why, we're
laughing all the time, make us weep, and you'll have a *lot*
of coins. And he worked, and worked well, and all we did
was laugh—all except one, Queen, that I know of—myself! One who wept bitterly from the beginning of the
great Clown's work to the end of it, and fell to the bottom
of his soul with grief and admiration at the Clown's re-
fusal of our coins, and the forefeiture of his shoe. Myself,
and more than likely Jamie, too. *(Pause.)* And more than
likely each of the others, too, each of us unwilling, Queen,
unwilling to let the other know of his pity and love for
his Father. *That* is why.

QUEEN. I thought it was for the child.

BOSS. No. I have my own, know them and love them and understand them, and don't understand them, and probably never will. It is for the Father. The King. The Madman. The Clown. The *Father* of the Child. *(He gets up suddenly, speaks softly.)* I must go along here now and study the problem. *(He goes.)*

(The GIRL *looks around at everybody, goes to the* BEAR, *rests her head on his shoulder, then turns and runs out.)*

FATHER. *(Shouts.)* Gorky, I wish you'd stop liking only pretty girls!

CURTAIN

ACT TWO

SCENE VI

Early Monday morning. The FATHER *is up. The* MOTHER *is up. The child is in her arms. The* BEAR *is waiting. The family suitcase is packed. The* QUEEN *is up. The* KING *is up. Everybody is doing little things in silence. Making bundles, folding things, tying shoelaces and packages.*

KING. Well, Queen.

QUEEN. Yes, King.

KING. Monday.

QUEEN. Yes, Monday. The first day of the week.

KING. And the last day of the World.

QUEEN. Oh, stop.

KING. Do you know it's the name of the theatre, *actually?* I found out only yesterday, out front.

QUEEN. I had no idea. In any case, you've got both your shoes, and I've got all my things.

KING. And we've eaten well these past few days.

QUEEN. Yes, we have.

KING. There's another theatre that's been dark for years. *(Points.)* A little up, and east.

QUEEN. Oh, no, no.

KING. Where, then?

QUEEN. Where all the others are. I don't mind.

KING. Alone?

QUEEN. What a strange question, King. What a strange word. Who can be alone?

KING. You can. I've seen you alone when I've been right beside you. Alone?

QUEEN. Yes, I think so.

KING. Well, let me carry your bundle until you're there, at any rate. I've nothing of my own to carry.

QUEEN. *(Sweetly)* Would you? Just until I'm there? (KING *smiles.)*

I've never understood such places too well. Where they are, and how one obtains entrance.

KING. It's the same with me, of course, but I'll ask, and we'll find out.

FATHER. You're both welcome to come with us.

QUEEN. You're very kind. Oh, no, thank you.

MOTHER. We'll do very well. I know we will. There will be plenty for all of us, and we *need* your help.

KING. The Duke *might* have learned to wrestle the Bear, or the other way around.

FATHER. Yes, yes, that would have helped a lot.

KING. *(Looks up and all around.)* Well—

(FOOTSTEPS are heard, and then a KNOCK at the door. The KING *opens the door, and there in the doorway is the* DUKE, *and behind him the* SILENT BOY. *They come in.)*

DUKE. *(Looks around, nodding to each.)* Well, here he is. Where's the Girl?

QUEEN. She left soon after you did. She went out to find you.

DUKE. I've been looking for this Boy. He can't speak, but he *can* understand, and I've told him the Girl loves him.

QUEEN. Boy? Do you love the Girl?

(The BOY *looks at the* DUKE, *then back at the* QUEEN, *then nods one nod.)*

Well, she's been gone for several days now. But she's somewhere about. Look for her. You'll find her. Because she'll be looking for *you.*

(The CREW BOSS *comes in, walking slowly and thoughtfully, followed by* JAMIE, *with papers in his hands: charts, floor plans, and so on. The* BOSS *nods at everybody, looks up at the problem. He looks at his watch.)*

KING. We're ready. We're on our way, and thank you very much.

BOSS. *(Goes to the* KING, *looks at him intently.)* Good luck, Father. Good luck, all.

(He and JAMIE *go.)*

FATHER. *(To the* DUKE.) Join us. We need you. We'll be working the streets at first, but soon we'll get to the circus, I'm sure.

(The DUKE *thinks about this, but does not reply. The* FATHER *and* MOTHER *smile at the others awkwardly, and nod, and the* FATHER *unloosens the* BEAR'S *chain. They begin to go.)*

QUEEN. Oh . . .

(The MOTHER *stops.)*

May I have one last look at the child, please?

(The MOTHER *hurries to the* QUEEN, *who looks intently at the child, then nods, and the* FATHER *and the*

BEAR and the MOTHER go, all of them waving, including the BEAR.

DUKE looks around, bewildered because the GIRL is gone. He looks up. The SILENT BOY nods, and turns to go. The DUKE stops him, shakes his head, looks up. They ALL wait in silence. The GIRL comes in through the open door.)

GIRL. I've come back for my man, if he'll have me.

(The DUKE turns and looks at her. The GIRL runs to his arms. The DUKE puts one hand at the back of her neck and the other at the back of the BOY's neck and holds them in place, staring at one another, speechless. Slowly, little by little, the DUKE draws them together, and they embrace. He looks up.)

DUKE. Thank you, sir. *(He turns and hurries out.)*

(After a moment the KING and QUEEN embrace the embracing BOY and GIRL, and then gesture at them to get along. They go, with their arms around one another.)

QUEEN. All right, King. *(She looks around and up, smiling.)*
KING. I'll be along in a moment.

(The QUEEN smiles at him, turns and, walking like a queen, goes out. The KING looks around, too, and then out into the auditorium.)

KING. Farewell, then—womb, cave, hiding place, home, church, world, theatre—a fond and loving farewell. *(He works the yo-yo.)* Farewell, and welcome! *(He waves to the theatre, and goes walking swiftly.)*

CURTAIN

END OF THE PLAY

ABOUT THE PLAY

AN IMAGINARY INTERVIEW
ABOUT A NEW PLAY

The New York Times, Sunday, October 13, 1957

MALIBU, Calif.

Let's say somebody—anybody—is asking a playwright questions about a play.

Let's say the play is "The Cave Dwellers" and the playwright is William Saroyan, at his home on the beach in Malibu, on Tuesday, Aug. 27, 1957—six or seven or eight weeks before the opening of the play at the Bijou on Forty-fifth Street, in New York. Let's say it's half past five, receding tide, blue sky, hot sun, Joe Gould recently dead in New York, the playwright done with the day's work, standing on the back porch, looking at the sea again, and the sky, and the white clouds, and the sea gulls, and three small girls with their baby brother on the beach, where it's wet only when the tide comes up and just barely reaches their feet, making the little boy laugh and jump. Let's say all that.

Anybody: I'd like this interview to be earnest and informative.

Playwright: O. K.

Anybody: What did you write it for?

Playwright: Posterity and my enemies.

Anybody: You're kidding already. Please try to keep it earnest. This is a time of sorrow in a world of trouble.

Playwright: Wise guy. The posterity I speak of is yesterday's, which is here. My enemies are my friends.

Anybody: I'll let that pass. *When* did you write it?

Playwright: I began writing it on January 1st, 1955, which was a Saturday.

Anybody: When did you stop writing it?

Playwright: On January 8th, another Saturday.

Anybody: Isn't that a rather brief amount of time in which to write a play? Eight days?

Playwright: Not if you're a playwright and have a play to write. If you are, and if you have, it's a *lot* of time. More time than anybody else might be likely to suspect.

Anybody: Eight days is eight days.

Playwright: Not to the man who's writing a play. To him it's time itself. *All* time. Gone, coming, here, and gone again.

Anybody: I think we had better change the subject.

Playwright: O. K.

Anybody: You haven't had a play on Broadway since 1943. You've been saying for years that you wouldn't have a play on Broadway until you could produce and direct it yourself. How come Carmen Capalbo and Stanley Chase are producing it?

Playwright: It's a miracle, and I believe in 'em.

Anybody: Capalbo and Chase?

Playwright: No, miracles. I believe in Capalbo and Chase, too, although a little less than in miracles. I had no intention of not sticking to my long-range plan until I asked the opinion of an unbiased bystander.

Anybody: Who was the unbiased bystander?

Playwright: Maybe I shouldn't have mentioned the matter.

Anybody: No, it would be quite informative if you named who it was who advised you.

Playwright: I had a man out to paint this back porch. He wanted to know what kind of work 1 do. I told him. He told me to let a play-producer have one of my plays.

Anybody: Why?

Playwright: I don't know. He was so sincere that I decided I'd better. That's how it happened.

Anybody: Well, I guess we'd better change the subject again.

Playwright: O. K.

Anybody: What's the play about?

Playwright: That's not for me to say.

Anybody: Leonard Lyons says Oscar Levant says everybody in every one of your plays is decent. Nobody's dirty, nobody jumps up and down and screams, nobody stabs his mother with a can opener, nobody takes cocaine, nobody studies at the Actor's Studio, nobody wants injustice eradicated once and for all by organized and systematic protest, demonstration, alcoholism, free love and riot.

Playwright: Boy, that was pretty good—what you said.

Anybody: Is it true?

Playwright: It's a lie. Georgie Americanos in "Love's Old Sweet Song" took a phony telegram to an old maid just to get even on another messenger. I've got other characters who are Bad Guys, too. Laughers, I mean. They laugh all the time and don't really care about the human viciousness other playwrights begin to attack midway in the first act.

Anybody: And yet you're not an idiot.

Playwright: No, sir.

Anybody: Then, there *is* a reason why you write plays the way you do.

Playwright: No, sir.

Anybody: There *must* be.

Playwright: There must?

Anybody: Of course.

Playwright: In that case, I guess there is, but it can't be *much* of a reason. I really wouldn't care to make anything of it.

Anybody: But what is the reason?

Playwright: I am.

Anybody: How do you mean?

Playwright: My poor old Daddy. My poor old Mammy. I guess they didn't hate me. I guess maybe they even liked me. I was a little shaver, then, of course. And so if anybody's to blame, it's got to be me—that is, *them*. Daddy and Mammy. But most likely their Daddies and Mammies liked them, too, so it's not easy to know who to blame. If it's all right, I'd like to blame Mr. Bernard Baruch.

Anybody: Why?

Playwright: I don't know. For not hating me, I suppose.

Anybody: Didn't Mr. Baruch hate you, either?

Playwright: No, sir. If he had, I might have been impelled to have more Bad Guys in my plays. I might even have had them *all* bad.

Anybody: What for?

Playwright: To help?

Anybody: Help who?

Playwright: Oscar Levant?

Anybody: Are you asking or answering?

Playwright: Leonard Lyons?

Anybody: Time to change the subject again.

Playwright: O. K.

Anybody: Is the play going to be a hit?

Playwright: Yes, sir.

Anybody: Is it going to become an industry, like the other plays that are hits?

Playwright: No, sir.

Anybody: Well, is it or isn't it going to be a U. S., Broadway, boxoffice, ticket-brokers' hit?

Playwright: No, sir, it's going to be the same kind of hit all of my plays are.

Anybody: What kind is that?

Playwright: Not hysterical, and not greedy.

Anybody: I don't understand.

Playwright: Ever listen to Mozart?

Anybody: Yes.

Playwright: Ever understand Mozart?

Anybody: Yes.

Playwright: Good.

Anybody: One last question. Do you like the drama critics?

Playwright: Why? Don't they belong to the human family?

Anybody: I mean, do you think they've got any brains?

Playwright: How much brains do they need?

Anybody: Do you think they'll have enough brains to recognize "The Cave Dwellers" as a real play even if it turns out that there isn't even one little old lousy Bad Guy in it?

Playwright: I'm sure they will.

Anybody: What makes you think so?

Playwright: None of them has a criminal record.

Anybody: Well, thank you, anyway.

Playwright: Joe Gould should have finished writing "The Oral History of the World." One American publishing house should have had one man who could talk to Joe in Joe's language and gotten him to write it and keep writing it. The publishing house should have published it, and lost money, and kept publishing it, and lost more money. Now, Joe isn't talking any more, not even his own language. Too bad. The poor nation has lost another treasure.

OPENING NIGHTS I HAVE KNOWN

Cue, October 19, 1957

The night of the opening of my first play, "My Heart's in the Highlands," at the Guild Theatre on 52nd Street, early in 1939, I wasn't in New York. I was either on a train in the mountains between Mexico City and Vera Cruz, or on a ship bound from Vera Cruz to New York. In any case, I didn't know the play was being performed. I wasn't there. I felt fine, both on the train and on the ship. When I reached New York I learned that the play had opened. Several of the drama critics had liked it, especially George Jean Nathan and John Mason Brown. Several had liked some of it but had found most of it confusing, and several had hated it, as the saying is. I thought I would go and see it and find out for myself what it was that was happening on the stage. I saw it. It hadn't been cast the way I would have cast it, it hadn't been directed the way I would have directed it, but on the whole it was pretty good. I haven't yet seen a performance of it that I have especially liked, however. Most people connected with the theatre have no sense of the theatre. They are just there, as the fulfilment at last of a bitter determination to *be* there. Such people become the great producers, directors, and actors. They do not become the great playwrights, however.

The opening night of my second play, "The Time of Your Life," in September of 1939, in New Haven, I was in the theatre, fresh from San Francisco, because at the last minute my cousin Ross Bagdasarian had wired me that I had better have a look at the play right away because (he implied) it didn't look right. I had written a small part into the play for him, because he had come up to San Francisco from Fresno and had announced that he wanted to be in the play. I had sent him to New York with the part and a letter, and he in turn had sent me the warning telegram. What I saw on the stage in New Haven was not "The Time of Your Life." Whatever it was, only one audience (or at the most two) saw it. If strange performances could be collected as strange books are, that performance would be a collector's item. I won't bother to go into details, but what I saw taught me just about the most important thing I could ever hope to learn about the theatre in general and my own playwrighting in particular: a play is achieved or miscarried on the boards by its director; it is more his play than it is the playwright's; he has got to put himself into it, unless the play is what I call a lumber play, a play of wood in its ideas and in its people, in which case nobody is required to put himself into it.

I took over the directing of the play. It opened on October 25th at the Booth on 45th Street, I believe. There was another opening that night, too: something adapted from a novel by Dostoyevsky, so I bought a ticket to the gallery to that play, and watched it until the arty hysteria drove me out of the theatre to the Automat for coffee and a doughnut.

The opening night of my third play, "Love's Old Sweet

Song," with Walter Huston, late in the season of 1940, I believe, I wandered around in the streets, and every now and then stepped into the theatre to find out where the play had reached, and to listen a moment to the audience. That was a time when most New York intellectuals, as they are inaccurately called, found it fashionable to join the Communist Party, or half-join it, or to affect having joined it, and to regard anybody who didn't happen to agree with them, and possibly didn't even like them, as a Fascist.

The play was a lark about human pretending, pride, pomposity, and pitifulness. I had staged it well, and it was being performed expertly. Huston's performance, as always, was magnificent, and I kept timing my visits in order to catch his best moments, because frankly they made me laugh. In the play was a "migratory worker" from Oklahoma or Arkansas, his wife, and his twelve or thirteen children. Arthur Hurnicut was this character, and Doro Merande his wife. Alan Hewitt was the *Time* Magazine man who tried to get them to subscribe while they camped on the front porch and roof and in the yard of the house of a maiden lady, played by Jessie Royce Landis. Well, every time I took a look at the play, I knew that all of our hard work in Philadelphia and in Baltimore had not been in vain. Every moment I caught was flawless. Every player, including the kids, was better than he had ever been. I was satisfied and grateful, even though I knew the play was a flop. How did I know? Well, standing in the back I could see and hear the audience. While I laughed, they hissed and said *fascist*. The play had a very short run. It is one of the best plays in the American Theatre. I wrote it, I staged it, I saw it performed, I ought to know.

My fourth play, "The Beautiful People," opened at the Belasco in 1941. I produced it with my own money, $11,000. I cast it, I directed it, I had Sam Leve design the set for it. When it opened I went to a movie. I offered anybody his money back at the boxoffice if he wanted his

71

money back, no questions asked. A few students took me up, and I was glad they did, because they had never before been able to buy orchestra seats. It had a good run. A lot of people saw it several times. I could have closed it with my own money doubled, but I kept it going until the $11,000 had been used up.

My fifth play also opened at the Belasco, sometime in 1942. It was called "Across The Board On Tomorrow Morning." With it was a shorter play called "Talking To You." I produced and directed these two plays with my own money, too. I didn't go to the opening night. The production flopped.

My sixth play, "Get Away, Old Man," was produced and directed by George Abbott. It is the only opening night of any of my plays I have ever gone to. At the end of the second act everybody connected with the play expressed the opinion that it was not only a hit, but a play that would get all the prizes. I said it was a flop. It was. They had misunderstood the reactions of the audience. That was in the fall of 1943.

From that year to this I have kept my plays away from Broadway, waiting for the time when I might produce them with my own money again. In May of this year I decided that I might never again be able to do that, and so I allowed another of my plays to appear on Broadway: "The Cave Dwellers."

It is scheduled to open on Saturday, October 19, eighteen years almost to the day after "The Time Of Your Life." I don't expect to be at the opening. I don't expect to be in New York.

(I didn't. I wasn't.)

THE REVIEWS OF THE PLAY

A SUNNY TALE

By Brooks Atkinson

The New York Times, Monday, October 21, 1957

On Broadway fourteen years have passed since William Saroyan last invited us to sit down to listen to a story. "The Cave Dwellers," which opened at the Bijou on Saturday evening, is one of the most enchanting stories he has ever told. Very likely, thousands of listeners will be sitting down to it all season.

Fairy-story would probably be the exact description. For "The Cave Dwellers" records the adventures of some penniless people who are camping out on the stage of an abandoned theatre that is about to be pulled down for a housing project on the East Side. One who calls herself "the Queen" is the ruin of a former actress. "The King" used to be a celebrated clown. "The Duke" was once a prizefight champion. "The Girl" (she is too young to have been famous at anything) is a homeless, frightened wretch who comes in off the streets.

Don't expect a plot or a conclusion from Mr. Saroyan. He is not the man to write with a slide-rule. But expect more humor, grace, innocence and improvisation than he has put in one piece since the halcyon days of "The Time of Your Life" (1939). Although food is scarce and the cold is congealing, Mr. Saroyan's characters have glowing spirits and wonderful memories of their triumphant days.

In the course of a newspaper review, it is a little difficult to explain how it happens that the cave dwellers are joined by a young man, his wife, baby and a performing bear. But it is part of the magic of the Saroyan style that a performing bear becomes a valid member of the community without straining the audience's credulity. No one is much astonished when he comes lumbering in. He turns out to be one of the finest creatures in the play.

If "The Cave Dwellers" seems to be the most winning play Mr. Saroyan has written in eighteen years, Carmen Capalbo deserves a share of the credit. As director, he has understood the play. He has cast it imaginatively. He has designed a performance that is as spontaneous as Mr. Saroyan's style of writing. The acting is a joy in every respect, and so is Bernardo Segáll's musicalized make-believe.

All honor to all the players—Barry Jones, whose droll comedy and perfect taste make the King a lovable figure; Eugenie Leontovich, whose guile, skill and animation make the Queen entertaining with an undertone of mockery; Wayne Morris, whose simple-hearted Duke is attractive and real; Susan Harrison, whose unaffected portrait of the Girl has strength, radiance, variety and depth.

It is the virtue of Mr. Capalbo's performance that it always has substance even when the writing seems capricious, and all the parts are acted freshly. For instance, Gerald Hiken as the trainer of the bear; his enthusiasm and confidence in the wrestling scene have tenderness and reality. Or Ronald Weyand's bear: without being cute it is full of personality. Or Clifton James and Ivan Dixon as the advance guard of the wrecking crew in the last scene: Their tone of concern and good will is just rugged and deliberate enough to make the sentiment of the scene palatable.

If the taste of the performance, and of William Pitkin's cavernous scenery and Ruth Morley's rag-bag costumes were not perfect, "The Cave Dwellers" might be mawkish

74

or might collapse in whimsey. But the theatre has taken Mr. Saroyan on his highest level as an original story-teller in a mood of good feeling. It is a pleasure to watch excellent actors make interesting characters out of his sunny improvisations. It is a pleasure to sit down to his sunny tale.

THE CAVE DWELLERS

By WALTER KERR

New York *Herald Tribune*,
Monday, October 21, 1957

One of the eleven sequences in "The Cave Dwellers" is taken up with a wrestling match between a man and a bear. The other ten are taken up with a wrestling match between William Saroyan the artist and William Saroyan the good-hearted, soft-headed evangelist.

Here are some of the falls that go to the artist:
Barry Jones, shivering in the patched-together clothes of a once-great clown, reports that he has been begging pennies of some men on a wrecking crew. He has wagered his decrepit right shoe against their pennies that he could make them cry. He has failed. They have refused the shoe, and offered the pennies, anyway. He has insisted that they take the shoe, and come home barefoot through the snow to beat his head against the walls and cry, "If I had lost my art, I did not want my shoe!" The moment, beautifully played by Mr. Jones, has an odd and genuine dignity.

Eugenie Leontovich, cocking her bobbed and graying hair restlessly as she kicks her heels over the footlights and counsels a love-baffled youngster, remembers a part she has once played in a terrible play. But she played it, and played it for more than a despairing and drunken playwright realized was in it. Miss Leontovich, like her author, knows quite a bit about the quirks and kinks and defiant mysteries of the creative process; she tosses them at us in firecracker profusion.

76

A milkman who has just had a whole basket of his wares stolen from him slowly and silently enters an abandoned theater. He sees five or six shabby people standing waiting for him, neither fear nor protest on their faces. He looks into their faces, discovers a mother and baby lying quietly on an old Cleopatra couch, discovers his stolen milk. Without a word, and without the least trace of sentiment, he goes. Actor John Alderman holds the sustained pantomime perfectly taut.

If all, or even half, of the evening at the Bijou were as composed and as compelling as this last fragment, the original Saroyan might be firmly back on Broadway. The point of the episode may be bald and obvious: rarely has the "milk-of-human-kindness" motif been so literally dramatized. But at least it is dramatized; it is part of a situation, it speaks for itself, it happens.

The balance of the entertainment, however, is in the very busy hands of Saroyan the prophet, Saroyan the juicy-fruit spieler. "The boy began in hunger," shouts the father of the baby, going on to explain that the mother was once his own meat and drink and is now the baby's milk. "A man is a father—I'm not a father—when I was a father my children were never born" says someone else, clearing up very little.

Echoes of "Waiting for Godot" and "The Skin of Our Teeth" keep cropping up, never to Mr. Saroyan's advantage. These destitute people are waiting through a long night ("What night is this?" "The night of our life.") A wrecking crew is coming closer and closer; outside the wind howls, animal cries are heard at the door.

And love is with us until it runs out our ears. The secret of the theater is love. To actors, even to hate is to love. "The sudden violence in me was love." Love is getting along into another day. There is, in short, more love to the square line in "The Cave Dwellers" than even the most amorous customer is apt to embrace. And it is, unfortunately, all in the lines: it never seems to reflect any actual state of heart in the huddled characters.

The players, under Carmen Capalbo's rather hushed but otherwise effective direction, are fine. In addition to the special conquests of Mr. Jones, Miss Leontovich and Mr. Alderman, there are attractive, doggedly sympathetic performances from Wayne Morris as an ex-fighter, Susan Harrison as a rain-drenched Alice in Wonderland, and Gerald Hiken as a little man with a big bear. Bernardo Segáll's carnival music is most helpful.

But Mr. Saroyan isn't listening very much these days. The echo of life goes down before the onrushing sound of his own benevolent voice.

SAROYAN'S LOVELIEST PLAY, THE CAVE DWELLERS ACTED MAGNIFICENTLY

By John Chapman

Daily News, Monday, October 21, 1957

Bless William Saroyan for being a dauntless sentimentalist, and bless all of the actors who are speaking for him at the Bijou Theatre. His play, "The Cave Dwellers," which opened Saturday evening, is a work of tenderness and beauty, and it has been magnificently staged by Carmen Capalbo.

It is best not to pry into the structure of "The Cave Dwellers" too closely, lest it crumble like a paper ash. When Saroyan writes he just lets himself go, and discipline would be the ruination of him; he must be taken for what he is—a poet with a loving heart who sings of the lowly of the human race. No matter what pitiful, shabby corner he pries into, he finds beauty there.

The locale he has pried into in "The Cave Dwellers" is indeed shabby, and it has been magically evoked by the scene designer, William Pitkin. It is an abandoned theatre on the lower east side, the only remaining structure in a vast jumble of demolition. Soon it, too, will tumble beneath the pricks and blows of the wreckers.

But now, in this time of bitter winter, the stage is occupied by a shivering collection of strays who have made pallets on boxes and covers out of threads and shreds of ancient draperies. To them the reaches of the auditorium, where I sat in thrall Saturday evening, are empty. They are playing out their lives to nobody but themselves.

They are indeed a Saroyanesque group and they all are

"of the theatre." They are dominated by the King and the Queen, whose ragged raiment is a reminder that once they were stars—he a great clown, she a great actress. With them is a hulking, simple ex-prize fighter, who is permitted to qualify because boxing is a kind of show business. They take in a homeless girl, pretending solemnly that she is an actress because she can recite the school-child's pledge of allegiance to the flag. They are joined by an unconquerable optimist who has a trained bear, a wife and a baby which was born in the stage doorway.

They are quite wonderful, these people, as they shiver through the last day of the old theatre. They share the pennies the King has begged and the milk the pug has stolen; they share their memories, hopes and loves. And when the wreckers come at last they go into the snow outside. Somehow there is hope for them, for their hearts are beating warmly.

The performances are without exception magnificent, with Barry Jones as the tragic jester, Eugenie Leontovich as the dimmed-out star, Wayne Morris as the simple and affectionate ex-fighter. Susan Harrison made little impression on me when I saw her in the film, "Sweet Smell of Success," but she captured me completely in "The Cave Dwellers." She is a young actress of extraordinary sensitivity. Gerald Hiken's performance as the bear trainer is another very fine one, and there are many more—including that of Ronald Weyand as a very realistic bear.

Ruth Morley's costumes are masterpieces of proud shabbiness and Lee Watson's lighting is a subtle performance in itself—and there are some extraordinarily evocative snatches of music by Bernardo Segáll. Saroyan, the author of "The Time of Your Life," has given us his most beautiful play. A realist might say of it, "Why don't some of these people go out and get a job?" If they did there would be no play. And perhaps Saroyan is writing of a time when there were no jobs . . . or won't be any.

THE CAVE DWELLERS
ARE SAROYAN FOLKS

By Robert Coleman

New York *Mirror*, Monday, October 21, 1957

William Saroyan loves people, and says so out loud. He is a master at getting eloquence from the inarticulate. Few dramatists of our time have his genius for characterization. He has a soaring imagination, and can put wings on words, though he sometimes uses too many of them—to the point of confusion.

In "The Cave Dwellers," Bill arrives at the notion that people are angels, and wonders why they have to dwell in caves and even human bodies. The cave, in this instance, is the stage of an abandoned East Side theatre, which shelters a once-great actress, a former top-flight clown and a broken prize fighter. They are identified as the Queen, King and Duke.

To their grubby haven have come a frightened girl, an animal trainer with a pregnant wife and a huge black bear, to escape freezing on icy streets. The child is born, and the fighter becomes a thief for the first time in his life to get milk for it. The milkman's son, a mute, chases him to recover the loot, and, seeing how things are, leaves it.

Eventually, a hard-boiled wrecking-crew boss wanders into their squatters' quarters, bent on demolishing the building to make way for a slum-clearance project. Softened by their plight, he orders his men to take a couple of days' sick leave, so that the refugees might have time to find other homes.

To be honest with you, we had a lump in our throat and moisture in our eyes, as these hapless, bewildered, yet valiant, folk, one by one, vanished through the theatre's

81

grimy and cobwebbed stagedoor. We felt as though we were parting, for the last time, from good and worthy friends. Philosophers and gallants, all.

Barry Jones is immensely touching as the clown who wagers a cast-off shoe against his ability to make strong men weep. All to gain coffee and a few coins. When he loses, the pride in his art is gone. He is almost destroyed. Yet, ironically, though he doesn't know it, he was more successful that he thought.

Eugenie Leontovich is moving, indeed, as the passé star who lives on memories. Wayne Morris is disturbingly accurate as the gentle pug, who missed a title because he was afraid of killing opponents with his punch. Susan Harrison, a young actress of quality, is warming as the girl who drifts into a seeming madhouse, only to find that it all makes sense.

Carmen Capalbo has directed Saroyan's parable with an eye for all its values.

It took courage for Capalbo and Stanley Chase to mount "The Cave Dwellers" at the Bijou. For we suspect that it is a motley fabric of frustration, hope and dreams, likely to have limited appeal. But, for all its faults, we found it enchanting. We're just a sucker for Saroyan. He's a man with a heart, God love him!

WILLIAM SAROYAN RETURNS TO US

By Richard Watts, Jr.

New York *Post*, Monday, October 21, 1957

It is good to have William Saroyan back in the theater; good for our enjoyment and also good for our souls. His new play, "The Cave Dwellers," which opened Saturday night at the Bijou, lacks some of his old-time exuberance of humor and prodigality of invention, but the basic Saroyan touch is still there, with its honest friendliness of spirit, its warm open-heartedness, and its utterly unpatronizing fondness for the misfits of the world. There is something wonderfully comforting about having it with us again in this day of our uncertainty.

Sweetness, benevolence and affection for the human race can be perilous commodities in the drama, and Mr. Saroyan doesn't make it any easier for himself by pushing them to the border of what a foe could call sentimentality. But he happily has a quality that turns his love affair with mankind into a beautiful romance instead of a vulgar liaison. It is his remarkable ability to make his fondness for battered humanity seem real and healthy and joyful; as utterly lacking in affectation or condescension. It therefore becomes completely winning.

In "The Cave Dwellers," the pattern is pretty much as usual. A group of outcasts with the gift of eloquence is huddled together in defense against the outside world, with an abandoned theater taking the place of the memorable barroom of "The Time of Your Life." They include an old clown, a veteran tragic actress, a battered ex-pugilist, and a gentle girl waif, but later they are joined by other Saroyanesque figures, including a trained bear.

And it is typical of the author that, when the terrifying outside world finally enters, it, too, is friendly.

But all of this, of course, is merely the framework for the true concern of the evening, which is the settling down of the dreams, the memories, the hopes and the fears of its people. And how appealing Mr. Saroyan makes this outpouring of their lonely spirits! He can even give us a speech in which the old actress insists that "the secret of the theater is love," an argument that is open to considerable debate in the case of certain other playwrights, and make it seem not only convincing but also a kind of ringing new slogan for the drama.

I guess it wasn't until that splendid bear, name of Gorky, made his entrance that I was completely captured by the spell of "The Cave Dwellers." For it seems to me true that a certain mellow sadness has taken place of the wild comic exuberance of the earlier plays, and I wasn't altogether sure that I welcomed the change. But the Saroyan heart is still there, and there is much to be said for the new mellowness. He has told us the theater's secret, and I'll tell you his. He makes us believe in his beautiful people because he believes in them.

That fine actor, Barry Jones, sets the tone of the play by his moving portrayal of the sad old clown, while Eugenie Leontovich, as the tragedy queen, and Wayne Morris, as the broken-down fighter, are splendidly right in their roles. There is an honest, touching and beautiful performance of the waif by young Susan Harrison, already an actress of quality in her first Broadway appearance. The others, too, are excellent, with a particular word due Clifton James as the sympathetic man from outside. It is all very cheering. Welcome back, Bill!

GRACE AND LOVE IN
SAROYAN STYLE

By JOHN MCCLAIN

New York *Journal-American,*
Monday, October 21, 1957

William Saroyan's latest dramatic venture, "The Cave
Dwellers," which opened at the Bijou Theatre Saturday
night, is a warm and emotional exercise in symbols. As in
his "The Time of Your Life," he is examining the world
and its often-tragic, frequently-funny and persistently-
baffled inhabitants. He comes to a sort of over-all conclusion that Life is grace and courtesy and love.

Along the way there are numberless other thoughts and
fancies which the audience can interpret in its own terms.
There will be those who see in it a pattern for world peace;
others, perhaps lowering their sights, will read into it a
simple exploration of human nobility. Whatever the con-
clusions, it cannot fail to challenge and stimulate the
serious theatre-goer.

To tell his tale Saroyan has assembled a weird cast of
indigents, living in a Manhattan theatre which is about
to be torn down. There is an ex-clown, now reduced to
begging, a former leading lady of the theatre, and a one-
time heavy-weight champion.

They are joined by a destitute young couple, complete
with new-born babe; an enormous black bear and his
trainer; a young lady fugitive from a toy factory, a young
man who works for the milk company, and sundry others.

There is utterly no point in describing what they do,
since the play follows no conventional pattern. They sleep
and dream, they come and go in the slow parade of their
struggles for survival. They hope and despair and love;
they have small successes and failures.

But they are never dreary. The writing is almost always bright and beguiling in the Saroyan manner, and it is occasionally very funny. This is the idiom of the people, and it has a true ring. There are also three songs, composed by Bernardo Segáll, wonderfully-well integrated into the mood of the proceedings, and ingratiating in themselves.

Barry Jones, that superlative performer, has a field day in the role of the broken-down clown; Eugenie Leontovich is appealing, hilarious and constantly commanding as the former star of the theatre; Wayne Morris is a surprisingly studied and relaxed one-time prize fighter. As the young girl, Susan Harrison gives a poignant and wistful performance.

There are other capable assists from: Gerald Hiken, Vergel Cook, John Alderman and Ivan Dixon. William Pitkin has supplied a setting of an empty stage converted to a dwelling which is suitably shabby, and Carmen Capalbo has ingeniously utilized his people and the novel medium to notable advantage.

"The Cave Dwellers" will have, in my opinion, a limited appeal. It demands respect and thoughtful consideration from its customers, and the public willing to make such an effort seems woefully wanting these days.

On the other hand, it's a gratifying experience—for the devout.

SAROYAN EYES LITTLE LIVES

By Frank Aston

New York *World-Telegram and Sun,*
Monday, October 21, 1957

William Saroyan in his "Cave Dwellers" arranges a dozen performers (including a tiny dog) in two acts and 11 scenes to illustrate some of his ideas on mankind. They are gentle ideas, quizzical, baffling and softened with laughter. They reach no stunning solutions, but that's because Mr. Saroyan doesn't pretend to be his brother's caretaker. He is content to look on with tolerance.

His cave is the strewn stage of an abandoned theater on New York's lower east side. It is about to be razed in a slum clearance project. Existing in the cold gloom are a discarded prize fighter, a forgotten leading woman, dubbed the queen, and the shell of a one-time clown, known as the king. All have tasted greatness, all now look less than nothing, but in each burns a wry, comical, pathetic yearning to be helpful, to be applauded.

The king and queen have crept into this cavern because their kind of royalty belongs in the theater, "last arena in which all is always possible." They have admitted the ex-pug because he in his way has entertained. He, as the show starts, welcomes a wispy girl seeking shelter from the snow and from life. And first thing you know, in come a man, his wife, a trained bear (played by Ronald Wey- and, let it be hastily explained) and an infant who is being born as the first-act curtain falls.

If you suggest this sounds a little jumbled and irrational, Mr. Saroyan might ask for any spot in life that does make sense. He's not reporting logic. He's entertaining with sequences that are important to the participants but actually little more than trivia. Even his boy-gets-girl is different. The two meet, fall in love and embrace without a word. It must be that way, because he's a deaf mute.

The play reeks with symbolism. The bear represents hurt trust (once and once only his master slapped him); the infant is a force to bring out the continuing goodness in people; the boxer is humanity groping for guidance; a lost shoe is vanity. A dream passage warns us not to let ambition and disappointment prey on our minds. Or at least that's what your observer derived from the thoroughly enjoyable rigamarole.

Acting and direction are superlative. In the forefront are Wayne Morris' lovable boob of a boxer, Eugenie Leontovich's actress who can still preen, Barry Jones' sad clown, Clifton James' heart-of-gold foreman. The incidental music, written in contemporary mode, fits beautifully.

Something pretty wonderful hit Broadway when the comedy opened at the Bijou Saturday evening. She played the maiden fleeing life's storm. The name is Susan Harrison.

SAROYAN IN A HARD SELL

By Walter Kerr

New York *Herald Tribune,*
Sunday, October 27, 1957

I find myself in the unhappy position of picking on the man who picks on nobody, William Saroyan.

With his first produced play in fourteen years, "The Cave Dwellers," the irrepressible Mr. Saroyan is offering us a sort of affirmative "Waiting for Godot." In a musty old theater building that is just two inches away from a slum-clearance wrecking crew, three very tired troupers are waiting through "the night of our life" for a morning that will be followed by another night and then by another morning, and nothing more.

One of them, testily and triumphantly played by Barry Jones, is a long-out-of-work clown who apologizes for a bitter, stomping tirade with the remark that "I might have gone on forever out of loneliness and despair" and who, at the end of his life, must forlornly conclude that the red and white makeup he used in his youth was his real face, while the battered countenance he now owns is the mask.

Another is an aging actress, a faded prop rose pinned to her moth-eaten sweater, who defiantly crawls from her couch for "the one good hour every day" that is still in her, and who—in the restless, snappish, often exhilarating playing of Eugenie Leontovich—is able to piece together a vivid memory of past glories ("I was very good in that part"). The third, gently and humbly outlined by Wayne Morris, is a prize-fighter whose constant prayer has been "Help me to win without killing my opponent" and whose fear of injuring another human being has led him to defeat.

The trio is joined, as the backstage shadows rise and fall, by a pale, wide-eyed girl who wants to be taken in by someone, somewhere, and by a wandering family of street-performers that includes a very small baby and a very large bear.

All that is asked of any newcomer who wants to rest for a moment in this last-ditch refuge is that he once have entertained somebody: the girl narrowly gets by because she can pledge allegiance to the flag and shakily sing "How do you do, my partner?" All that Mr. Saroyan asks his desolate but undefeated figures to do before they are at last forced out into a snow-covered alleyway is to love one another. There may be no intelligible future for these abandoned good folks; but they are good folks, and their goodness will keep them warm.

It does keep them—and the theater itself—warm in odd, intuitive, heart-lifting flashes. When Mr. Jones is politely but just a shade grimly asking that he be allowed to swear for a moment, or crying out that he is a very proud clown, or interrupting his own run-on despair to suggest names for the baby, irony and pity are curiously, touchingly welded. There are passages in which Miss Leontovich gaily accepts the irrationality of life, love and art, in which Gerald Hiken leaps into the arms of his trained bear and speaks approvingly of the bear's theatrical know-how ("The weather was against us" is the animal's explanation for their failure), in which a milkman and a construction foreman come to cavil and stay to help—passages that leap forward across the footlights with instantly-acquired authority.

And there is, at the very end of the evening, a swiftly established mood of regret, resignation, and quiet leave-taking that is for a few elusive seconds—stunning. The vanquished leave, one by one; the theater's worklight is slowly carried to center stage; a silent summary says that the people are going, the building is coming down, and a light is still burning in one long-drawn, rhythmically perfect, breath. A sigh is made visible.

The very moving image is, however, rather wantonly

spoiled by Mr. Saroyan in a manner that has dogged him, stubbornly, throughout eleven scenes. Just as we are completely immersed in the unnamed atmosphere, the author decides to name it. His clown must stop, turn to us, and shatter the spell by speaking. Nor does he speak in the glancing, bemused, leftfield scraps of overheard life that his author can manage so well, when he isn't trying. (Consider the faint, falling, infinitely evocative "I'm not mentioning any names, Pa, but something's wrong somewhere . . ." that serves as signature for that small masterpiece "My Heart's in the Highlands.") Instead he speaks pontifically, in the overheated urgency of a philosopher who isn't quite sure his remarks have been profound enough and is going to make them more profound by repeating them, louder.

Indeed, Mr. Saroyan seems to me to have brought a cleaver down on his play, splitting it at the heart, by his steady insistence on defining, rather than simply displaying, the passions that move him.

The sentence beginning "Love is . . ." occurs more times in eleven scenes than I could count, try though I did. The ensuing definitions are various, but they have certain things in common: they are rhetorically written by the man in charge rather than affectionately teased from the characters, they are precariously close to cliché, they delight in paradox because paradox sounds well even when it has no discernible point, and—this is what hurts most—they never really support, or further, the actual emotional relationships that are fitfully lighting the stage. When one of the fugitive figures at the Bijou is reporting an actual experience—let's say he has been chased through snow-covered ruins by a milkman's son and is disturbed because the chase made no sound at all—the effect is wonderfully graphic; when the same figure is forced to speculate mystically on the nature of fatherhood ("When I was a father, my children were never born") the effect is simply arid.

The charge that has most often been leveled against the author of at least two of the contemporary theater's most enchanting improvisations is that he has never truly disciplined himself; absence of discipline has usually been associated with Mr. Saroyan's no-sequitur narratives and unpredictably prankish characters. With "The Cave Dwellers" it strikes me that we've been looking for the wrong skeletons in the wrong closets. Mr. Saroyan's irreverence for tidy theatrical form is probably a virtue; most of the conventions are breaking up these days, anyway. The characters from outer space—or wherever it is they come from—are obviously a delight.

Where Saroyan is indulging himself is in the pretentious and intrusive language of the sponsor's commercial; he wants to tell us all about those rich, beneficent vitamins instead of just letting us taste them. And, in the telling, he has the same choked-up sales-appeal sound to his voice.

The actress he has himself created is, in her theatrical instincts, a bit more sensible. "When you're cold," she says, "it's better to have a fire than a philosophy."

ALL THE ACTORS HAVE GOOD
MATERIAL IN IMPROVISED PLAY

By Brooks Atkinson

The New York Times, Sunday, October 27, 1957

Welcome home, Bill Saroyan! Since no one writes more at random, no one can waste more paper and ink over a period of time.

But when everything falls miraculously into place in one of his scripts and when the right stage people take charge of the performance, no one can be more disarming and refreshing. Since 1939, when "The Time of Your Life" enchanted the town, and 1941, when Mr. Saroyan produced "The Beautiful People" under his own direction, he has been prolific, as usual, in all forms of prose, not to mention song-writing. But "The Cave Dwellers," now at the Bijou, is the first of his plays in many a long year to convey satisfactorily the warmth, good-will and spontaneity of this most undisciplined of writers.

When he fails in the theatre, he is not always altogether responsible. Our naturalistic theatre is not equipped to deal with his artless fancies. Most acting and direction are too literal. But Carmen Capalbo, who stylized "The Threepenny Opera" so brilliantly, has found the key to Mr. Saroyan's effervescence in the stage direction. He has put a frame around "The Cave Dwellers"; he has given it a solid foundation and made a free-verse stage poem out of a modern fairy story.

If Mr. Saroyan sets the actors serious problems, he also rewards them with wonderful scenes. During the course of the evening each of them has the stage to himself and at least one effective scene to play. Barry Jones plays the part of a great circus clown who is now penniless and living with other congenial derelicts on the slovenly stage of an abandoned theatre on the East Side. Among Mr. Jones' admirable qualities is the impression he gives of always acting. There is an aura of theatre around the parts he plays. He is not the character he is playing; he is an actor playing the character, commenting on it silently out of his own amiable intelligence as an artist.

His seedy clown in "The Cave Dwellers" is perfect. And nowhere more so than in the scene in the last act when he is explaining how he lost one shoe to an unappreciative audience of building workers and at the same time is proposing suitable names for a baby that has just been born. There is no logic in this double dialogue; it is one of Mr. Saroyan's tours de force. But Mr. Jones gives a limpid performance that mixes humor and sadness in the manner of the old Chaplin movies.

Three years ago Eugenie Leontovich was playing the elegant, regal grand duchess in "Anastasia." Now she is playing a ragged old crone who was once an illustrious actress. Nothing could be less prepossessing than this stringy-haired, thin, unkempt, messy pauper. But the second act contains a scene in which Miss Leontovich, sitting on the edge of the stage, recalls a part in which she gave an electric performance many years ago. Out of the ruin come images of magnificence. Out of the misery comes grandeur. Out of the clutter and sloppiness comes style. It is wonderful, and Miss Leontovich knows it.

So it goes throughout a vagrant tale of vagabonds: every actor has his moment. Susan Harrison, a gifted young lady making her Broadway debut, has a chance to break everyone's heart when she sings a nursery rhyme and pledges allegiance to the flag to prove that the character she is playing is really an actress and belongs in the company of actors. Wayne Morris, as a former prizefighter, has several winning scenes. In the best of them he explains how he stole a dozen bottles of milk and why he will not resist arrest when the law comes to the door. There is a certain nobility in the way Mr. Morris plays it.

As the trainer of a performing bear, Gerald Hiken has a poignant comedy scene in which he tries to teach the bear how to wrestle with the prizefighter without injuring him. Mr. Hiken plunges into the scene with the eagerness of a salvationist. In the last act, Clifton James appears as the boss of a wrecking crew that is going to evict the squatters and demolish the old theatre. This could be a colorless, utilitarian scene designed merely to conclude a rambling play. But Mr. James plays it with such candor, manliness and honesty that it gives the whole play a fillip. It contributes something positive to the cheerful mood of "The Cave Dwellers."

For nothing has been done carelessly in the performance Mr. Capalbo has directed. The music, the movement, the scenery and costumes, the lighting, have the delicacy and taste of a fairy story told without cuteness. Mr. Capalbo has neither patronized it nor improved upon it.

In the program Mr. Saroyan declares, among other things that are less acceptable, that the theatre is "the last arena in which all is always possible." The touching, shining performance of "The Cave Dwellers" bears him out. This autumn the Broadway theatre has begun on a harsh note. "West Side Story" is relentlessly tough-minded. "Look Back in Anger" is mordantly negative, and "The Egghead" was devastatingly sardonic. "Miss Lonelyhearts" was savagely bitter. Since the negative mood reflects the realities of today, it is valid.

But here comes Mr. Saroyan bearing his familiar gifts of kindliness and innocence. Like Sholom Aleichem, he loves the poor as the children of heaven. "The Cave Dwellers" is an engaging fantasy about some social cast-offs who have not become embittered. In the course of five days they do not have enough to eat to keep a fly alive. But they are lively people with pure spirits. They never surrender their belief in one another.

For they are all different aspects of the writer who invented them out of himself. All these years Mr. Saroyan has been writing at top speed—win or lose, sink or swim. The quality of his work varies remarkably. But through it all he has never ceased being Bill Saroyan, a good egg and an original teller of tales.

FROM *THE NEW YORKER*

By WOLCOTT GIBBS

November 2, 1957

The unhappy critic confronted with a play by William Saroyan, the well-known Armenian cornucopia, is in a most peculiar situation. If he chances to be against the work, he is also instantly supposed to be against a great many other things, including truth, beauty, golden-hearted eccentrics, delicate fantasy, and, especially, love. The reason for this is that in the public mind Mr. Saroyan, in addition to being a playwright, has come to be the living symbol of practically everything that is brave and warm and tender, agreeably sad but at the same time irresistibly gay. To condense this thought to more manageable dimensions, Saroyan *is* love, and anybody who doesn't like love is a coarse and cynical scoundrel, and obviously deserves to be boiled in treacle. There is, naturally, the matter of degree to be considered. That is, the critic who doesn't like Saroyan (or love) at all, who finds the plays only whimsical in the most damaging sense of that word, and even somehow softly repellent, is clearly a full-scale scoundrel, to be cooked accordingly. The critic, on the other hand, who is about equally divided between fascination and boredom, who is aware that a poetic imagination is at work but simultaneously regrets that it is being put to such paltry and undisciplined uses, is merely half bad and should suffer no worse fate than simmering for a little while, gently, in some thin, clear soup. My own position, in regard to Mr. Saroyan in general and to his new play, called "The Cave Dwellers," in particular, lies somewhere between these two. I was irritated by what I considered labored and foolish invention and boozily pretentious prose for about two-thirds of my visit to the Bijou and delighted the rest of the time by the author's happy inspiration and the simple felicity of his writing. This makes me rather more a scoundrel, or conceivably a son of a bitch, than not, and though I don't know what the penalties for that condition are, I am prepared to accept them with resignation.

"The Cave Dwellers" is not a play that lends itself readily to synopsis. The action takes place on the stage of an abandoned theatre on the lower East Side that is threatened by a wrecking crew, already blasting away next door. The characters present at the beginning are a pair of down-and-out but indomitable actors, known as the King and Queen, and an ex-heavyweight boxing champion, sometimes called the Duke and sometimes just the Man. Presently, they are joined by a waif (The Girl), who has lost her job in a toy factory and is accepted as a member of the sad but glorious company of public entertainers when she is able to recite the pledge of allegiance to the flag. In the course of the evening, this group is augmented by the arrival of a performing bear; his trainer; this man's wife, who has a baby in the intermission between the acts; a speechless young milkman, who has come to retrieve a case of milk that the Duke has stolen for the baby; and the foreman of the wrecking crew, accompanied by one of his workmen. The inhabitants of the theatre are all cold and hungry and destitute of rational hope, but they still have their dreams (appropriate, though not really terribly interesting, dream sequences are duly inserted), and, above all, they can still talk. Their conversation, which wambles along for the better part of two acts and eleven scenes, is, of course, concerned principally with love. Among other things, it is observed that love is the motivating force behind all human activities, including the theatre, a nation that might well divert the management of "Compulsion"; that it more than compensates for old age, poverty, and failure; and that it has no rational boundaries, a moth-eaten bear being just as easy to love as a beautiful woman, if you put your mind to it.

97

I am not yet sufficiently abandoned to say that I am indifferent to love, but I am obliged to admit that I am not stimulated by Mr. Saroyan's opinion of it. So much for that portion of the entertainment. The parts of the play I liked aren't easy to describe. There is the scene in which the young man comes to get back his milk and looks around, long and silently, at the people on the deserted stage and then leaves empty-handed; there is the one in which the old actor tells of the final failure of his art (he bet his right shoe he could move a gang of laborers, but they only laughed); and there is the fighter's gentle surrender of the Girl to the speechless boy. All these episodes are examples of the high level of genuine sentiment that Mr. Saroyan's talent can achieve, just as the introduction of the dancing bear is a nice example of his gift for agreeable absurdity. It is a great pity that "The Cave Dwellers" contains almost no others.

The company assembled to bring this version of Mr. Saroyan's habitual message to the public is headed by Barry Jones, as the King; Eugenie Leontovich, as the Queen; Wayne Morris, as the fighter; and Susan Harrison, as the Girl. They go about their work with enormous sincerity, charm, and—well, love. As for their supporters, I was strongly attracted to the actor named Ronald Weyand, who represents the bear, though I might note that no performer disguised as an animal has ever failed to bewitch me on the stage or probably ever will. The director, Carmen Capalbo, and William Pitkin, Ruth Morley, and Bernardo Segáll, who provided the set, the costumes, and the incidental music, in that order, are to be complimented, too.

THE SHOEING UP OF
WILLIAM SAROYAN

By Henry Hewes

Saturday Review, October 28, 1957

The happipest news of this theatre season is that in "The Cave Dwellers" William Saroyan has refound himself as an artist. One would guess that for him the past fourteen years were filled with self-doubt, injured pride, and the semi-conscious realization that his quixotic brand of escapism and wish-fulfillment was no longer effective in a world desperately staving off annihilation.

"The Cave Dwellers" begins by *recognizing* the tense current situation. Its curtain rises on three indigent ex-theatre artists living on the stage of a theatre which is about to be demolished by a wrecking crew. There is the King, a former music-hall clown, who used to be rich and "a wit in the world." His concern is for the home, the cave, the hiding place, "and not for the creature human or animal, lost out there, and lost in each of us—alone, piteous, helpless, near the end, and yet somehow deathless, indestructible, unkillable." While he is frightened of this outside world, he is willing to face a crisis alone.

There is the Queen, a sick old actress who used to play elegant roles. Although she is the child of a poor drunken father and his shrill wife, she has always been queenly, and can still pull herself together for an hour to seem young and beautiful again. When she joins the frightened family circle she stops coughing, but she prefers coughing to being afraid and wailing. The King says to her, "If Christ Himself had had you around He would have sold oranges for a living, Moses would have dealt in hides and leathers, and Mohammed would have written dirty limericks. All the others would have forgotten their visions and holy dreams." Her reply is, "They *should* have. If we are nothing involved in nothing, and wish to be something involved in something, let it be so. But quietly and plainly, not with hysteria and violence."

And there is the Duke, an ex-boxing champion who twenty-five years ago in his last fight was scared he might kill his opponent with a single blow, so instead let his opponent kill him with a single blow. He's always been stupid, but strong, swift, and lucky. Simply religious and Christian, he "fears himself named God." In an anxiety dream, he is counted out in English, German, Chinese, and finally in Russian.

Into these allies' hiding place runs a homeless girl who has lost her job helping to make guns for the U.S. Toy Company. She was dreaming of America as it is represented in the movies during work. She has no right to join the group because she is not "of the theatre," except that she can recite the Pledge of Allegiance to the flag.

The allegorically-minded may find in these riddles fading England, impoverished but elegant and free-thinking France, the naive but powerful United States, and the refugee. This foursome waits, not for Godot, but for the approaching wreckers. Comes the cold night, and a desperate knocking is heard at the door. The King doesn't want to open it, but he is outvoted by his humanistic allies. It is a man with a huge performing bear, and a wife who has just given birth to a child. Since the bear is named Gorky, we think of Russia, and since his master has his confidence we think of the working class in those countries recently become independent. The new father tells how the bear's soul turned sweet when it first saw his wife. The wife, then, may represent a good-life-for-all ideal, and the son the hopes for a universally better future. In "The Cave Dwellers" the new father tries desperately to make the bear and the boxer trust each other enough to play at wrestling together, rather than box, because one blow would cause Gorky to go mad and kill, but wrestling he would soon associate with friendship and love. Saroyan seems to see in this improbable wrestling match the hope of the world, but realistically has the new father fail to bring the Duke and the bear together.

The final crisis comes when the boss of the wrecking crew enters to blow up the theatre. He is touched by the situation and instructs his workers all to report sick in order to delay the demolition until the new family is able to move. Saroyan seems to be offering no short-range optimism, only the long-range hope that annihilation will be partial. But he does offer us stoic comfort in the words of the Queen: "I should be angry that we know nothing and that we cannot learn. But I am not . . . This is how it is . . . What's the world for? It's for putting up with— with grace. With pride even. Without excuses, without astonishment, without regret, without shame, without system and order—excepting grace and courtesy and— love. Right love and wrong, *any* and many."

The King adds that the human-being speaks, sings, laughs because "We *don't* belong here. It's a cave. What are we doing in a cave? We're angels. What are we doing in bodies? For some reason we are trying our best, hope-lessly, to pretend that we *are* in them, that we *belong* in them."

Fortunately, enjoyment of "The Cave Dwellers" doesn't really depend on such highly conjectural interpre-tation of its text. It lives on its compassion that surpasses understanding, and its humor.

As usual Carmen Capalbo's directorial hand seems weak, but also as usual he has several performers outdoing themselves and in a fresh way. Perhaps this paradox is mirrored by the Queen who, after telling of a bad play in which she had to portray a girl torn between several con-fused courses of action, adds, "I was very good in that part."

As the Queen, Eugenie Leontovich gives the truest-ringing performance of her career. She is a divine mixture of elegance, fire, and plain-speaking as she demonstrates Mr. Saroyan's thesis that the theatre is something stirring and coming to life in the soul of the audience, "a smile, a memory, a reminder of an old forgotten truth, tender regret, kindness, love." Equally memorable is Gerald Hiken, who as the new father gets a genuine vitality into his antics with the bear. Wayne Morris is the epitome of courtesy and gentleness as the Duke, and Susan Harrison is properly waif-like as the girl. In the difficult role of the King, Barry Jones is admirable though possibly less dynamic than he might be.

Saroyan has included a personal touch in the parable of the ex-clown who fears he has lost his art and is too proud to admit it. After withdrawing from action by risking and losing his shoe in a bet that he can make some workers both laugh and cry with his old act, he swallows his pride to reclaim his shoe. Saroyan has done likewise by now bringing us for better or worse the most honest and mature new play he can write. It's a triumph.

October 28, 1957

The Cave Dwellers are broken-down performers camping in a crumbling, abandoned East Side theater. A done-for boxer, a beat old clown, an ailing old actress are joined by a sweet young girl and a man with a trained bear and wife who gives birth to a baby. By day they lie abed, or street-beg, or in desperation steal milk. By night they act out their old roles, philosophize, soliloquize, dramatize the day's rebuffs, fall asleep and dream.

With his first Broadway play in 14 years, Saroyan is clearly back at the same old stand, making the same old pitch—but without his onetime showmanship. He was often soupy and boozy about the down-at-the-heel in the old days; but at his best, as in *The Time of Your Life,* he had an alcoholic gaiety and verve, and a real knack for brewing instant-vaudeville. The poet in him might slump or the philosopher babble, but the prankster sufficiently triumphed.

In *The Cave Dwellers,* Saroyan is no longer a high-spirited toastmaster to waifdom, but its long-winded poet laureate. There are the usual variety turns, but not much seems cockeyed or even imaginative. There are sad-eyed little gallantries instead; and even when Saroyan half-mocks at stage doings, he seems half-mawkish. His people are not just too good to be true, but mostly too good to be interesting. Their one message is love, love for one another; all is love, the secret of the theatre is love, even hate is love. All this, however devoutly to be wished for, not only remains fairly dubious as fact; it never soars as poetry, or gets moving as drama. Saroyan's words are too many and too vague; the dialogue, at moments, even sounds as if the actors were unsure of their lines. As it happens, the actors are extremely good. As staged by Carmen Capalbo, the production provides lift: Barry Jones makes a fine-flowing aria of his unhappiness, Eugenie Leontovitch a bright nonsense piece of her stage memories.

Theatrically, it would not matter if Saroyan wrote first with an eraser—to wipe out reality—if afterwards, with a pen, he created magic. But this play has little magic: only a stab of pathos, now and then, in a wilderness of plight; or a flash of color, humor, poetry amid constant murmuration.

SAROYAN PERSUADED BACK TO BROADWAY

The Cave Dwellers
Sets Forth Gently Comic Fable

BY JOHN BEAUFORT

The Christian Science Monitor,
October 26, 1957

Some time back, a disenchanted William Saroyan abandoned Broadway to its own haphazard devices. Carmen Capalbo and Stanley Chase have now wooed him back, which is a good thing for Broadway and, one hopes, for Mr. Saroyan. His gently comic fable, "The Cave Dwellers," at the Bijou Theater, demonstrates that he still writes with an individual freshness, spontaneity, and careless rapture which no one else has successfully approximated and only Mr. Saroyan has been able to imitate. Lately supplied with its share of drama which looks back or sideways in anger, the theater can stand a play that looks forward with hope.

In its own tentative and unmomentous way, that is what "The Cave Dwellers" does. It is a play about love, courtesy, kindness, and unselfishness. "Love is the secret of the theater and the art of the world," says one of the characters. It is the open secret of "The Cave Dwellers."

A Saroyan "note about caves and their dwellers" in the Playbill states, in effect, that all the world's a cave. He goes on to assert that his new play happens on the empty stage of an abandoned theater "because the theater is the cave at its best—the last arena in which *all is always possible.*" Like most other conventional iconoclasts, Mr. Saroyan dismisses the government and the church as hopeless. Pope's "the proper study of mankind is man" apparently suffices for him.

To quote further from Mr. Saroyan in Playbill:

"Two of the leading characters of the play, called the King and the Queen, are professional actors, old, unemployed, ill and comic, because apart from the truth that every man in the world is inevitably an actor of one sort or another, who else but rejected actors would find sanctuary on the stage of an abandoned theater, with a silent and empty auditorium? Who else would return with regret and hope to a fallen empire except a King and Queen driven long ago from their own realms?"

Who else in "The Cave Dwellers" include the Duke, an ineffably gentle ex-prizefighter, and the Girl, a homeless waif whom the Duke passes off as an ex-player in order to admit her to the shelter of the forlorn royalty. They are joined by a Father, Mother, their silent Baby, and almost silent trained bear. Having brought them together in this freezing refuge, Mr. Saroyan sets them talking about life and their problems as they await the wreckers who are scheduled to demolish the theater in the interests of a housing project.

Saroyan talk is not easily compressible (particularly by Mr. Saroyan). One may perhaps perform the reporter's office most unobstructively by recording that the goal of the talk is to penetrate with love the barrier of hopelessness and confusion. Here and there, a breakthrough is won.

Since Mr. Saroyan has steadfastly ignored all the critical tongue-clucking about his lack of literary discipline, he should not be expected to begin heeding it now. His major occupation is tuning in on the sad-sweet-comic music of humanity. His major discipline is driving himself to compose his own libretto for the score. Take it or leave it—lyricism, comedy, eloquence, banality, pseudo philosophy, and all.

When Mr. Saroyan's inspiration ignites, it gives a lovely light. At its best—such as in the King's heartbroken, outraged confession of his failure to entertain some workmen with either his comic or tragic powers; in the dumb show of a silent milkman as he enters, circles the stage, grasps the situation, and leaves without retrieving the milk the Duke has stolen from him; or in the Duke's touching love for the Girl and in his affecting prayer, "Help me"— in such moments, "The Cave Dwellers" becomes suffused in the wonder, emotion, and affection at which Mr. Saroyan is aiming.

Most of the best things in "The Cave Dwellers" happen in the second half. And many of the best moments are provided by Barry Jones as the King and Wayne Morris as the Duke. Mr. Jones gives a superbly appealing performance as the battered clown reduced to beggary. Mr. Morris' portrait of the intuitively sensitive and kindly prizefighter may quite possibly turn out to be the finest acting of the season.

As the Queen, Eugenie Leontovich's bravura flamboyance is not matched by a clarity of speech which is virtually essential to this involved and talky play. Susan Harrison projects the pathos but not the luminous quality required of the girl. Other roles are well played by Gerald Hiken as the man with the trained bear, Clifton James as the wrecking crew chief who gives the transients a reprieve and buys them food, John Alderman as the mute milkman who loves the girl, and Ronald Weyand as Gorky, the bear.

Mr. Capalbo's responsive direction seems almost too muted at times for the nature of the play. But undoubtedly the performance as a whole will achieve greater dynamics with repetition. William Pitkin's setting captures the fusty, mysterious glamour of an empty playhouse and Ruth Morley's costumes augment the atmosphere. Lee Watson's lighting seems over-subdued but Bernardo Segáll's music is attuned to the tone of latent theater magic.

FROM *CUE*

By Emory Lewis

November 2, 1957

—William Saroyan, after a long absence, is back on Broadway, this time under the auspices of the admirable Capalbo-Chase series at the tiny Bijou. Mr. Saroyan, in his chosen exile at Malibu Beach, hasn't changed much. He still loves love, and he still dispenses his own unique brand of whimsy and affection.

Mr. Saroyan is a man who engenders great passions in his viewers. Many go away enraged from any Saroyan opus, whether it be book, article, or play. Others find him the top of the morning. I find myself in a somewhat uncomfortable position—in the middle.

In "The Cave Dwellers," the playwright offers us a strange group of down-and-outers living in an abandoned Lower East Side theatre. Clown Barry Jones supports the ragged band by begging. He's the King. Eugenie Leontovich, who is often quite ill, is the proud Queen. She was once a celebrated actress. Wayne Morris, a battered ex-prizefighter, is the Duke. Along comes Susan Harrison, a waif frightened by the cruel world, and she becomes accepted as part of this little theatre group. She can recite the allegiance-to-the-flag bit, so that makes her of the legitimate stage. The group is finally joined by a family with a new baby and a trained bear. Somehow they all survive, an outpost of courage and grace and love in an indifferent world.

Often the script is quite obscure, and the stage seems flooded with irritating symbolism. Sometimes the author is merely garrulous. But now and again, he finds a way to one's deepest emotions with a brilliant sequence. When Barry Jones tells his little band how he forfeited his shoe in mid-winter to a group of construction workers because he couldn't make them weep, there is genuine pathos. The clown has lost his art, and there is no greater loss. When a deaf-mute milkman, strikingly played by John Alderman, comes to recover his stolen milk and decides to leave it all behind for the hungry group, one is deeply touched. Or when a wrecking crew foreman, beautifully portrayed by Clifton James, tells the benighted group he will help them, Saroyan's gospel of love dominates the tiny stage.

But there are many moments when the love is too much. You ask petulantly: sure, you offer sweetness but how about more light? A Saroyan play is something like being on a hazy pub-crawling binge. The world's absolutely wonderful. But the morning after, you begin to ask questions.

WAITING FOR SAROYAN

By Patrick Dennis

New Republic, November 4, 1957

William Saroyan has been absent from Broadway for 14 years. To me, at least, they have been 14 years of peace and prosperity with hardly anything "cute" being said or done on the stage. But now, concurrent with the drastic decline of the stock market, Mr. Saroyan has reappeared, to a salvo of rave notices, at the little, six-hundred-passenger Bijou Theatre, with a two-act comedy called *The Cave Dwellers*, which leans heavily upon *Waiting for Godot* and crushingly upon the theatre-going public's seemingly boundless sentimentality.

The Cave Dwellers is peopled by more Saroyan people than one would have thought possible. There are fey people, sad people, beautiful people, little people, lost people, brave people and absolutely *no* bad people. In fact, all people are, according to one of the characters, "angels who dwell in human bodies." Also present are such Saroyanesque fixtures as a performing bear, a mute milkman, a yo-yo and that standard stage bundle of rags hastily wrapped in a blanket and called a baby.

The story is roughly this: On the stage of a cold, deserted theatre—and a theatre that is about to be torn down in a lower East Side slum clearance project—dwell three lost, old people patiently waiting to die. They are The Queen, a fallen star, played with great verve by Eugenie Leontovitch; The King, who was once a great clown, performed floridly by Barry Jones; and The Duke, a broken-down prize fighter, done with beautiful sincerity and simplicity by Wayne Morris. Into their impoverished little derelict world come a lonely, lost girl; a destitute young couple who own a performing bear and who have a baby the instant they arrive; a mute young milkman from whom The Duke has been obliged to steal milk in order to feed the baby and its mother; and eventually the boss of the wrecking crew who takes pity on them and allows them a few days' grace before their world is demolished in the name of progress.

Knowing my Saroyan pretty well, I keep trying not to ask myself such questions as "With his wife in labor, why would a young husband take her *(and* a performing bear) through a blizzard to a derelict theatre instead of picking a nice warm hospital where more capable people might be on hand to attend the accouchement?" Or, if the time is the present, as Mr. Saroyan says it is, I wonder why it is that a beggar can get no coins per working day at a period when panhandling is fairly lucrative or why it is that just a couple of the characters can't find jobs. I try to fight down these mundane questions but it's a losing battle. And while these nagging little queries simply display my own mean nature, they also fire a bullet right through the big, beating heart of William Saroyan.

Happily, there are some very pleasant things to report about *The Cave Dwellers*. The performers are uniformly superb. Barry Jones, while a bit too rich for my blood, brings warmth and color and pathos to the fairly standardized role of the sad old clown. Eugenie Leontovich, as always, lends magic and majesty to the discarded actress.

Two refugees from Hollywood do impressive work. Wayne Morris proves that, once free of the virile-young-man parts imposed on him by the film studios, he is capable of a brilliant and moving performance. In fact, I found Mr. Morris' work the most noteworthy, possibly because his role is the least flamboyantly written. And Susan Harrison, whose screen debut in *The Sweet Smell of Success* did not shatter me, is lovely and affecting as the lost young girl.

John Alderman, whose mute milkman depends solely

upon pantomime, performs with both thought and restraint. While I was less taken with Gerald Hiken and Vergel Cook as the owners of a newborn son and a trained bear, they read their slightly mortifying lines with more authority and less embarrassment than anyone had a right to expect. The director, Carmen Capalbo, is also to be commended for leading his little band of players through the mawkish morass of Saroyan silliness with no fatalities. Bernardo Segáll has also contributed some incidental music that is haunting, catchy and wonderfully orchestrated for a modest group of four instruments.

One wonders how lesser talents might have fared at the hands of Mr. Saroyan. There are speeches as confusing as: "A man is a father. I'm not a father. When I was a father my children were never born." I guess I get it, but is it worth the trouble? There are speeches—this one explains how to bear a son of one's own—as distressing as: "Get with a man to get a man of your own." The actors are forced to call one another Man, Woman, Girl, Child, Mother and Father, as well as King, Queen and Duke. And the word Love pops up—often in triplets— at least a thousand times during the course of a seemingly long evening. It's love, love, love till you're sick, sick, sick. At least that's the way *The Cave Dwellers*—outstanding as its performers were—affected me.

But, as with all of William Saroyan's writing, your reactions will depend entirely on your feelings for the author's work. If you *don't* love, love, love Saroyan, stay home, home, home.

By Harold Clurman

November 9, 1957

I do not particularly admire Saroyan's *The Cave Dwellers* (Bijou) but I shall praise it.

I shall praise it because it is by Saroyan. He is a writer, he is a poet, he is a personality. Among our dramatists he is one of the few who speak in a distinctive voice. It is a gentler voice than that of most others who write for our theatre. It uses simple, sane vocabulary which refers to smells and sounds and easily identifiable things seen and heard. It is good humored, and slightly inebriate. It has in it a faint flavor of the foreign, yet it is unmistakably American. It reflects the genial aspect of San Francisco where the sea, the harbor, the market place are not over-whelmed by the great hotels, and where the small bars and restaurants have not yet been transformed into machines.

Saroyan's plays have something else that we cherish in the theatre: they have color and fancy—not laid on but organic to his message and his plots. His germinal ideas lend themselves to the *optique* of the theatre. Something in them calls for the magic of stage lighting and the imaginative costumer.

Most of these attributes are present once again in *The Cave Dwellers*. The design of the play is pleasing. A broken-down old actress, a used-up clown, an ex-pug, a pretty young waif, fired from her job in a toy factory, all seek refuge on the bare stage in a soon-to-be-demolished theatre. The three older people have made a little kingdom of their cold, shadowy haven. The actress is the queen, the clown the king and the pug the duke. They adopt the little girl, who becomes an honorary subject.

In their little world these people dream with pleasure or fear of their past, they seek out food for one another and they give shelter to a man who has trained a bear and whose wife gives birth to a child among them. The pug steals milk for the new-born baby; the milkman's apprentice, a mute but prince-like boy, allows these people to keep the milk and brings more because he recognizes their plight and falls in love at first sight with the waif.. They all entertain one another with shreds and patches of their talents and when the wreckers arrive—the wreckers too are kindly people—they all depart each his own way into the mysterious night.

What meaning informs this allegory? Its "philosophy" might be called sugared existentialism. We do not know why we are here, we cannot comprehend the universe we are in, we shall never understand the great pattern, if pattern there be, of life. No matter; there is goodness, there is love—even hate is love. We get up in the morning, go to bed at night; in between we play wondrously—and that is enough. We require no more, for the spectacle is bright and even the dark is light enough.

I do not scoff at this, because, for one thing, there is little difference, artistically speaking, between "Life is a dream," and "Life is real." Both propositions may be the seed of beautiful statements. I shall go even further and say that I share Saroyan's sentiments. But *The Cave Dwellers* is still not only slight but I'm afraid somewhat threadbare.

For goodness and love (at times the play reminded me of Chaplin's song about love-love-love-love) have significance only where there is a confrontation with pain and evil. You can have no goodness or true love without a full awareness of the *objects* which are the substance of life. The substance or material of life is always resistant and this resistance—the subject of drama—is what we have so much difficulty in accepting. Saroyan tries nonchalantly to eliminate life's negation: he waves pain away, as in one of the play's best lines, "My cough is simply a language I have not yet learned to understand."

The play—unlike *My Heart's in the Highlands* and *The Time of Your Life*—does not spring from any contact with reality: it is more pose than spontaneous reaction. Its wistful smile is painted on as on a doll. This "poem" is constantly explaining itself—which only a bad poem does. The language, though fluent, is exposition rather than speech. There is a thinness in the writing which comes from a lack of genuine dramatic impulse. As a result, much of what is said and shown, instead of being touching, becomes platitudinous. If there is wisdom here, it is only for hobos.

Yet the play is good enough in concept for us to wish it were much better. A really imaginative production would help. (It is my guess that, because of its remarkable stage potentialities, the play will be produced in many theatres abroad as well as in little theatres in our country.) Not that the present production is bad. The cast (which includes Barry Jones, Eugenie Leontovich, Wayne Morris, Susan Harrison, Gerald Hiken, Ivan Dixon) is in the main well chosen. These actors have nice qualities and act creditably. (I wish Leontovich would remain as simple throughout as she is in her better moments, for a queen—even a footlight queen—is always basically simple, not stagey.) What is missing is true style.

There are two possible styles for this play. One would seek that poetry of the spirit which is evoked when the soul of the actor as a person is stimulated beyond the surface truth of each scene. Another style might be created through delicately but frankly picturesque characterization and stage movement heightened with memorably graphic craftsmanship. At the Bijou, the actors are merely themselves in the least interesting sense of the word. And yet—such is our theatre nowadays—the show has freshness.

A WORD ON THE
THEATRE IN GENERAL

BY WILLIAM SAROYAN

The theatre has many problems, but none of them can kill it any more than human problems can kill the human race. As long as people continue to get up in the morning or whenever it may be that they *do* get up after sleeping, there will be a theatre, great or not, or great *and* not by turns, mainly not, of course, because greatness in art if not in life is uncommon.

Begin at the beginning, with the building: the enclosure, the playing area or stage, and the area for the beholders, or the auditorium: in a jammed city like New York all space is precious and has to be used cleverly, and so no one pretends that any of the theatres on Broadway (or off) are ideal. Seeing and hearing are not evenly apportioned among the beholders in any theatre in New York City. If it is in order for the people on the side or at the back to see the whole set and action, and to hear everything that is said, it is also in order for the people up front not to be so near that they cannot see the set and the action as a whole, or that everything they hear is in the form of shouting.

Films apportion seeing and hearing more effectively than the stage does, but the film-makers themselves keep their eyes and ears close to the stage in order to have new plays out of which to fashion new movies.

Watching a play on television is a different order of experience than watching a play in a theatre, or watching a movie, but each of these mediums *is* theatre. Each has its exterior, or non-art, advantages and disadvantages. During a play on television, for instance, it is entirely in order to go to sleep, or to move to another channel, or to shut the thing off, because the beholder is at home.

At a movie you can get up and wander around or shop in the lobby and go back and sit down and be none the worse for having been gone. If going to the movies used to be a religious or folk activity, the hysteria that sustains·a religion or the fun that sustains a folk activity are no longer as intense as they used to be, and most people can take or leave even the biggest and most ballyhooed movie without any particular feeling of loss or gain.

All the same, all three mediums are in business, all three are doing well, and are likely to go on doing well.

It isn't necessarily spiritual vacuity in people that impels them to use up a great deal of their time by going to the theatre in one of its three variations. Why they go is beside the point as far as this paper is concerned. They go.

The Armenians of Fresno tried to put up a building and to establish a theatre there about thirty years ago, but the project failed. At a money-raising meeting in the Civic Auditorium my uncle Garabet got up and said, "This project is foolish. How can you possibly expect Armenians to pay ten cents to sit in a crowded theatre and watch actors on a stage pretend to be human beings when there are always much more interesting things happening in every Armenian house, with plenty of space all around, good doors, and much more comfortable chairs? We know who we are. There isn't a soul in this building who isn't a better actor than anybody I ever saw on a stage, and they've got cleaner teeth, too."

The project, which had for several months taken on an artificial aura of patriotism, promptly fell to pieces and everybody in the auditorium resumed his career as an actor right where he sat. Only the professional actors felt that my uncle was a monster. The fact is they had planned to charge a quarter admission.

Failure to recognize one's own life as drama *does* probably account for some of the appeal of the theatre. Most people never suspect that they are in fact living an epic drama, or that they are characters in any number of small plays and in one enormous one. To consider one's self unreal or unworthy of the meaning art gives to real or imaginary people appears to be the unfortunate compulsion of most people, not in our time alone but in all time. Those who insisted that they were not unreal and not unworthy of artful meaning became the great actors, not on the boards of theatres, but in the world itself, although now and then a man who might have been great in the larger theatre chose to be great on the boards, perhaps because he had to have his applause immediately. Even when the applause was for effectiveness in an evil role, both he and his admirers believed that he was only performing, and wasn't actually evil at all. Acting was safe. If they had to hang you, you always left the theatre after the performance and went home to a nice supper.

Next comes the drama itself, the play. This is a difficult thing to talk about, but it has always been talked about, and always will be.

The indisputable truth is, there is no end to the *kind* of plays that *can* be written. But we must be concerned about the kind that *are*. They are very little things. They are anecdotes, jokes, episodes, fragments, little poems, little songs and dances, and they are certainly harmless if you don't think the essentially meaningless and useless and repetitious isn't harmful.

The fact that they are done on purpose, on schedule, gives them a kind of importance and meaning that sometimes comes to something or other, as looking at a few grains of sand through a microscope gives both sand and looking a new and perhaps greater order of importance and meaning.

Some of this piercing meaning on the stage comes from the writing, but if you want to understand how empty even the best writing for the theatre can be, recall a bad performance of *Julius Caesar*, and pretend that you didn't know who had written the play, or the reputation it had acquired. A performance of a condensed version of *Julius Caesar* by the graduating class at Longfellow Junior High School impelled me to regard Shakespeare as a bore, entirely without humor, unable or unwilling to notice that his whole theme was pretentious, not tragic. They didn't need to stab Caesar at all, and then they didn't need to feel miserable about it.

A great play needs great actors. What *is* a great actor? A great actor is a great person. Are there any great actors in the world today? There are a few.

The profession of acting attracts all sorts of people for all sorts of reasons. All of the people are good and all of the reasons are good, but few of the people are great or have the makings of greatness in them, and so the teaching of acting flourishes. How to stand and move and speak *can* be taught, of course, but greatness can't, and no real teacher pretends that it can. Still, the teachers point with pride to the achievements of some of their students, but the thing that really made their successful students successful was the poor competition and a part in a play.

In the twenty years from 1937 to 1957 the theatre in America has seen the arrival, and now and then the departure, of less than half a dozen fairly good playwrights, including the writer, who arrived in 1939 and departed in 1943: Odets, Miller, Williams. Surely there are others, but I can't think of them at the moment. Each is an American, each writes as an American, each has style and stature and skill, but altogether the America they suggest in their playwriting is less than one tenth of one per cent, as the saying is, of what is really there, both in the raw material of the time, the place, and the people, and in the potential of the play as an art form. Round up *all* of the plays written and produced from 1937 to 1957 and the figures aren't much improved.

You can't expect to have a theatre without playwrights and plays. You can adapt from novels, from comic strips, from labels off jars of instant coffee. You can take great court trials and quote from the manuscript. You can take great actors and fit something around them like a magician's cape. But none of this is playwriting.

How does it happen that a country like America, with all of its jive and jazz and juvenile delinquency, as it is meaninglessly called, doesn't produce more playwrights?

I don't know. More kids at college certainly go out for theatre than for football or baseball.

We are supposed to account for everything negative by humming about the threat of total destruction of the human race (by Russia, I presume), but the human race is still here, and those who are scared now were scared ten years ago, and ten years is a lot of time in anybody's life.

And how are we supposed to account for everything positive? Total destruction again?

If it's little moons that we want to launch because they're pretty out there, let's launch 'em, but I don't think they ought to scare playwrights. It is understandable that they might scare politicians, because they know they are the leading actors in a play that has no playwright and no director: performed in secret in a dozen different places. The play of the politicians has too much size, secrecy, and insincerity to have any real meaning or use. It involves multitudes, and art involves only a handful of people in a multitude. The politician doesn't really scare another politician far away, and he isn't really scared by another politician. Each of them scares himself. Caesar wasn't stabbed. He committed suicide. He didn't know how else to conclude his performance.

As science draws nearer to art, and as governments expose themselves, poets and scientists are likely to take the place of politicians in the human drama.

It is better to be a citizen of truth than of Transylvania, that purest and least laughable of governments.

THE CAVE DWELLERS

PROPERTY PLOT

ACT ONE

Pre-Set

Hat box L. of L. bed
Queen's coat, hat, shoes (D. L.)
Duke's coat, hat (D.R.)
Black scarf under pillow R.)
Bed U.C. on 2 low platforms, bedding
Bed R., bedding
Bed L., bedding
Pilot light U.S. corner bed (off; cord, plug)
Rag U.S. corner bed
2 chairs R.
Table R.
Tablecloth on table
Cupboard
 Stack 4 dishes
 Bear pan
 Jug on pan
Barrel U.R. corner trunk
Trunk U.R.C.
Costume coat on trunk

Clothes on line U.R.
Clothes line U.R.
Hatrack U.C.
Bed cover on platform U.C.
Umbrella U.C.
Onion skin and scripts in box U.L.C.
Theatrical labels on all trunks

Prop-Table off stage L.

Broom for Girl
Pumpernickel in bag
Coins
Cigar
Sugar
French bread
Knapsack
Queen's suitcase
King's bundle
Contents of wicker
 2 hats
 2 cymbals
 Coat

ACT TWO

Strike

Act One bread
Trunk dressing

Pre-Set

Water in shed

King's coat, hat, scarf on closed script box U.L.C.

Girl's coat on trunk U.R.C.

Empties D.L.

Wicker foot L. bed

Bag and string under L. bedding

Queen's coat on U.L. hook

Umbrella U.C.

Platform (Act Two setting)

Chair with padding U.C.

Sewing on chair (threaded long)

Baby on chaise U.C.

Screen in front of chaise

Trunk (new position)

Table (new position)
  Jug
  Bear pan
  4 dishes
  Cup
  Cup with milk
  Diapers
Barrel on R. chair
Pilot light on R. of R. bed
Black scarf under pillow
Bear chain, collar D.R.

Prop-Table off stage L.

Coins
Sugar
French bread
Knapsack
Queen's suitcase
King's bundle
Girl's ring
Yo-yo
Charts
Plans
Crate of milk bottles (1 real)

THE CAVE DWELLERS

COSTUME PLOT

DUKE:

  Lavender crew-neck sweater (torn at elbow and
      shoulder)
  Tan corduroy trousers
  Rope belt
  Sweat sox
  Work shoes
  Army overcoat (series 1943)
  Black and white checked cap

GIRL:

  Medium blue man's double-breasted topcoat
  Dark blue tam
  Faded light blue shapeless dress with fitted bodice
  Tan cotton knee-length stockings
  Black scuffed flat shoes
  Dark blue cardigan sweater

QUEEN:

  Deep maroon wool dress
  Gray wool sleeveless sweater
  Black wool knee-length stockings
  Maroon felt carpet slippers with rosettes
  Black wool coat with cape back trimmed with fur
  Black felt cloche hat with black ribbon

KING:

  Grey-striped collarless shirt
  Grey unpressed trousers
  Blue sox
  Black scuffed patent leather shoes
  Maroon sleeve-less inner sweater

Brown cardigan outer sweater (torn)
Black overcoat lined on inside with brown fur
Grey hat with black band (shapeless)
Brown and white checked scarf

DREAM SEQUENCE

ARAB:
White Arabian burnoose trimmed with gold (satin)
White abba headpiece with gold and black cord
White inner garment (muslin)
Gold shoes

WOMAN:
Blue cloche hat with blue feather
Blue fitted suit (jacket and skirt)
Blue pumps with high heels
Blue sheer stockings
Fox fur piece

YOUNG QUEEN:
White girl's party dress with lavender ribbon (circa
1910)
White hair ribbon

YOUNG MAN:
Black broad-brimmed flat-crowned Spanish hat
Black bolero jacket trimmed with black braid
White satin shirt
Black bolero trousers with flared bottoms
Black sox
Black shoes

FOREMAN:
Pink work cap with bill
Pink coveralls (U.S. TOY embroidered on back)
Pink sox
Pink canvas shoes

OPPONENT:
Gold boxing trunks

Gold boxing shoes
Gold boxing gloves

GORKY:

Realistic bear costume (black fur)
Detachable bear head with breathing tube
Detachable bear feet

FATHER:

Striped tan figured shirt
Blue sleeveless inner sweater
Faded green cardigan jacket
Brown shapeless trousers
Brown Army work shoes
Brown double-breasted overcoat
Brown airman's fleece-lined helmet

MOTHER:

Dark green double-breasted overcoat
Flowered yellow maternity blouse
Yellow knit boucle inner blouse
Black velvet inner skirt
Brown corduroy skirt
Brown denim outer skirt (wraparound)
Tan lisle stockings
Navy blue ankle sox
Brown loafer shoes

SILENT BOY:

White cap
White coveralls
Black turtleneck inner sweater
White sox
White shoes
White gloves

CREW BOSS:

Brown felt hat
Brown suede leather zipper jacket with knit cuffs
Blue work shirt
Grey moleskin work trousers
Brown wool sox

Brown work shoes
Brown leather gloves

JAMIE:
Yellow plastic construction worker's helmet
Grey inner sweat-shirt
Green and yellow checked wool shirt
Blue denim overalls with bib
Army combat jacket (olive drab)
Brown laced boots
Dark grey work sox

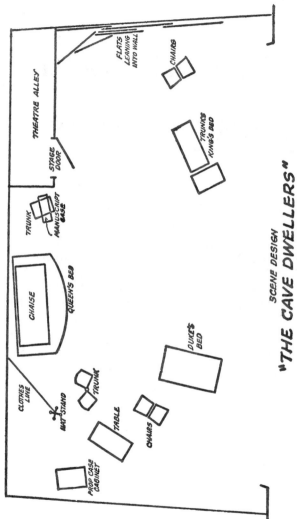

SCENE DESIGN
"THE CAVE DWELLERS"

NEW BROADWAY DRAMAS
from
SAMUEL FRENCH, INC.

AMADEUS – AMERICAN BUFFALO – BENT –
COLD STORAGE – COME BACK TO THE 5 &
DIME, JIMMY DEAN, JIMMY DEAN –
COMEDIANS – THE CRUCIFER OF BLOOD –
THE CURSE OF AN ACHING HEART – DO YOU
TURN SOMERSAULTS? – THE DRESSER –
DUET FOR ONE – EMINENT DOMAIN – FAITH
HEALER – THE GIN GAME – HEARTLAND –
I WON'T DANCE – KNOCKOUT – A LESSON
FROM ALOES – NED AND JACK – NUTS –
PAST TENSE – SCENES AND REVELATIONS –
THE SHADOW BOX – THE SUICIDE –
TO GRANDMOTHER'S HOUSE WE GO –
THE WATER ENGINE – WINGS

For descriptions of plays, consult our free Basic Catalogue of Plays.